Development in Conflict:
The Gender Dimension

Report of an Oxfam AGRA East workshop
held in Pattaya, Thailand
1–4 February 1993

Judy El Bushra
Eugenia Piza Lopez

Oxfam (UK and Ireland)

First published by Oxfam UK and Ireland in 1994
This edition transferred to print-on-demand in 2007

© Oxfam UK and Ireland 1994

ISBN 0 85598 294 2

A catalogue record for this publication is available from the British Library.

All rights reserved. Reproduction, copy, transmission, or translation of any part of this publication may be made only under the following conditions:
- with the prior written permission of the publisher; or
- with a licence from the Copyright Licensing Agency Ltd., 90 Tottenham Court Road, London W1P 9HE, UK, or from another national licensing agency; or
- for quotation in a review of the work; or
- under the terms set out below.

This publication is copyright, but may be reproduced by any method without fee for teaching purposes, but not for resale. Formal permission is required for all such uses, but normally will be granted immediately. For copying in any other circumstances, or for re-use in other publications, or for translation or adaptation, prior written permission must be obtained from the publisher, and a fee may be payable.

Available from:
Bournemouth English Book Centre, PO Box 1496, Parkstone, Dorset, BH12 3YD, UK
tel: +44 (0)1202 712933; fax: +44 (0)1202 712930; email: oxfam@bebc.co.uk

USA: Stylus Publishing LLC, PO Box 605, Herndon, VA 20172-0605, USA
tel: +1 (0)703 661 1581; fax: +1 (0)703 661 1547; email: styluspub@aol.com

For details of local agents and representatives in other countries, consult our website: www.oxfam.org.uk/publications
or contact Oxfam Publishing, Oxfam House, John Smith Drive, Cowley, Oxford, OX4 2JY, UK
tel +44 (0) 1865 472255; fax (0) 1865 472393; email: publish@oxfam.org.uk

Our website contains a fully searchable database of all our titles, and facilities for secure on-line ordering.

Published by Oxfam GB, Oxfam House, John Smith Drive, Cowley, Oxford, OX4 2JY, UK

Oxfam GB is a registered charity, no.202918, and is a member of Oxfam International.

CONTENTS

Foreword   v

I DEVELOPMENT AND CONFLICT: THE GENDER DIMENSION

1   Understanding Armed Conflict   3
1.1 Introduction   3
1.2 Analysing conflicts   4
1.3 Conflict as a process   13
1.4 A new model of development   13

2   The Gender Dimensions of Armed Conflict   19
2.1 Introduction   19
2.2 Women's experience of conflict   20
2.3 Changes in gender relations: power, conflict and transformation   32

3   Implementing Gender-Sensitive Responses to Conflict   39
3.1 Introduction   39
3.2 Assessment, monitoring and evaluation   39
3.3 Policy considerations in specific conflict-related situation   44
3.4 Partnership issues   46
3.5 Institutional issues   48

II CASE STUDIES

A.   The Impact of Armed Conflict on Gender Relations   55
1 Cambodia   Pok Panhavichetr   55
2 Somalia   Judy El-Bushra   58
3 Uganda   Judy El-Bushra   61

B.   The Effects of Conflict on Women   67
4 An overview   Claudia Garcia Moreno   67
5 A checklist   Gigi Francisco   74

C.   Meeting the Support Needs of Women in Conflict Situations   79
6 Sri Lanka   Nalini Kasynathan   79

D.   Working with Partners on Gender Issues in Conflict Situations   85
7 Burma   Shona Kirkwood   85
8 Philippines   Arlene C Mahinay   87

E.   The Evolution of Oxfam's Gender Strategy in Conflict   95
9 Lebanon   Lina Abu Habib   95

REFERENCES   98

FIGURES
Fig. 1: Types of conflict   11
Fig. 2: Situations of conflict   12
Fig. 3: Summary: key issues in understanding women's experience of conflict   31
Fig. 4: Different perceptions of power   35
Fig. 5: Checklist: assessing needs in conflict situations with a gender perspective   40
Fig. 6: Possible components for an Oxfam strategy for working with partners on gender and conflict   49
Fig. 7: Institutional factors in enhancing gender sensitivity in conflict responses   52
Fig. 8: The effects of conflict on women   73
    Table 1: Percentages of women who were victims of traumatic events
    Table 2: Protective index

FOREWORD

This report arose out of a workshop entitled Development in conflict: the gender dimension, which was held by Oxfam's Action for Gender Relations in South East Asia (AGRA East) network for East Asia (AGRA East) in Pattaya, Thailand, from 1-4 February 1993. Around 30 participants attended, drawn from Oxfam UK/I's Asia and Middle East programme, Oxfam House and members of the Gender and Development Unit), and from Oxfam's sister organisations in the region.

The purpose of the workshop was to consolidate work on gender and conflict which had been going on in Oxfam since 1988, but which had not been sufficiently integrated into the overall debate and research on conflict. It aimed to explore participants' own experience and expertise in working with women in conflict areas and to provide practice in the use of gender-sensitive methods of analysis and needs assessment. As such, the workshop was a groundbreaking experience, not only advancing the evolution of Oxfam's conceptual framework on conflict but also developing methodologies and practices which can be built on in future workshops.

In preparing the current report, the aim has not been to present a faithful record of the Pattaya workshop, but rather to reflect the spirit of the discussions in a form from which participants and others who were not there may be able to gain insights, and use in concrete ways. Some of the ideas discussed at the workshop have been further refined, and additional background material added. It is hoped that some of the material presented here will be seen as suitable for use in other workshops.

The report aims to be of interest to development workers (both in the field and in planning and policy positions) who are seeking practical and theoretical insights into problems they face in integrating a gender perspective into conflict-related work. In this respect the report has certain limitations.

Firstly, it assumes that readers are familiar with the Gender and Development approach, both as a framework for analysis and as a set of policy priorities in support of women. It does not argue the case for focusing primarily on women rather than on men, but aims to redress the imbalance in conflict work by which women's issues have tended to receive insufficient attention. As a result, women's suffering in times of war, as well as the contribution they make to their community's survival, has been unacknowledged, undervalued, and perhaps increased. In addition, lasting distortions in gender relations which may have long-term detrimental effects on a community may be underestimated.

Secondly, the report does not attempt a full analysis of armed conflict, which is a huge subject and quite beyond the scope of this paper. Though Part I presents an overview of the subject in order to place the rest of the discussion in context, this section does not pretend to provide a complete picture. It aims instead to complement work on development and conflict which has been emerging over the last few years, and to ensure that gender issues are centrally placed on conflict agendas.

In geographical terms, the main focus of the report is on South-East Asia, drawing as it does on the experience of workshop participants from the region. The report does, however, aim to have wide relevance. Experience from Africa and Central America has been integrated as a complement to the South-East Asian focus.

Part I of the report is divided into three sections: section 1 presents a tentative approach to understanding conflict in different Third World situations. Section 2 describes the impact of conflict on women and on gender relations at different levels of analysis. Section 3 discusses implications for NGO work, looking at research and planning tools, implementation, and training.

Part II consists of country-based case studies looking at different aspects of the question of gender and armed conflict: the impact of conflict on women's lives and identities and on gender relations, the evolution of appropriate NGO responses, and different approaches to working with partners.

Full details of the workshop, together with notes on exercises and on methodology, are available from Oxfam's Gender Team, for those wishing to replicate or adapt the Pattaya workshop.

I.1 Understanding Armed Conflict

Section 1 presents a tentative approach to understanding conflict in different third world situations

Women in a health clinic – Afghanistan

I DEVELOPMENT AND CONFLICT: THE GENDER DIMENSION

1 UNDERSTANDING ARMED CONFLICT

1.1 Introduction

Development agencies have been responding to the plight of civilian populations affected by conflict since the beginning of their existence. Indeed, many — like Oxfam itself — originated in the need to support refugees from war situations. So why has the issue of conflict and development taken on a renewed urgency in the 1990s?

First, conflict is no longer an exceptional circumstance. During the 1970s and 1980s, structural poverty deepened in the Third World, and the ending of the Cold War opened up outlets for local animosities, frustration, and rebellion, to be violently expressed in country after country. Increasingly, those involved in Third World development are finding their efforts checked by the impact of war. More and more, development workers are discovering the need to understand and address the root causes of conflict as well as to provide immediate assistance to those affected.

Secondly, non-governmental organisations (NGOs) are becoming increasingly aware that conflict is not an isolated issue; rather, it feeds off, and in turn nourishes, other factors of turbulence which have also become pervasive elements in the development landscape. These include environmental degradation, political inequality and repression, economic decline, and the growing scarcity of subsistence resources. Similarly, the complexities of conflict must be understood in the context of interrelationships within regional and global political systems, and wider world events. Armed conflict, then, currently stands at the centre of the concerns of agencies working with issues of poverty and injustice.

Finally, it should be noted that warfare in the latter half of the twentieth century has involved increasingly high levels of civilian casualties. UN estimates put the proportion of civilian casualties globally since the end of World War II at 95 per cent, compared to 5 per cent in World War I and 50 per cent during World War II.[1] Warfare used to be waged between the professional armies, in formal battlefield settings with regulated rules of engagement; in contrast, most of the 150 or so wars that have taken place since World War II have been internal conflicts in Third World countries. These conflicts are characterised as expressions of competition over shrinking resource bases in the context of the declining power of marginalised, impoverished states.[2] Violence is, in this context, a means whereby groups express their cultural identity and aspirations.

This shift towards the involvement of non-combatants in warfare can be seen both in the technologies of war (the scatter-bombs, the mustard gas, the anti-personnel mines) and in the growing use of anti-humanitarian practices of war. Of these practices, the denial of food, the destruction of agricultural land and other environmental resources, forced migrations, and 'ethnic cleansing' are among the most dramatic examples. Rape, which has been used over many centuries as a deliberate strategy in war, has now been recognised as a major abuse of human rights, both in conflict and in peace-time. Yet rape in contemporary conflicts is occurring on an unprecedented scale.[3]

Conflict leads to the breakdown of political structures and of economic systems, to productive land lying idle and cattle destroyed, to flights of displaced people and refugees. It is a process that heightens women's vulnerability. Development workers are faced with the consequences of conflict for the communities that are engulfed in such crises, and have to try to work with them in seeking innovative and creative solutions to the massive problems that they face.

This report seeks to offer insights into the connections between conflict and gender at the end of the twentieth century, arguing that such a gender analysis of conflict can contribute in two ways to our hope of understanding what prospects exist for future peace.

First, there needs to be a sustained effort to clarify the broad analysis of conflict processes and the factors affecting it at a global level. Gender approaches offer insights into this, addressing questions of power, control, competition, and models of development in economic, cultural, and political terms.

Secondly, there must be a clearer focus on the individuals and communities that are caught up in such conflicts: their motivations and reactions, their survival strategies, and the ways in which they manage to rebuild their lives and restructure their communities. Gender considerations are critically important here, helping to synthesise the analysis of the private (individual and household) and the public sphere (community and state).

Finally, it should be emphasised that looking at conflict through the eyes of women (as well as men) is essential in understanding the social network of survival and reconstruction in the aftermath of war, and in helping NGOs determine how — and in support of whom — they should respond to conflict. Gender analysis can operate at three levels: firstly, the theoretical approach of identifying gender differences; secondly, the practical focus on specific forms of gender imbalance and ways of righting them; and, thirdly, the strategic transformation of gender relations to provide a basis for justice and equity, not just between men and women but between different groups within society. Armed conflict can be pictured as a fault-line running across the evolution of a society, expressing injustice and grievances and often indicating where transformation is most sorely needed. At the same time, conflict and its aftermath may open windows of opportunity, enabling women and men to redefine the parameters of their lives, and put the past behind them.

1.2 Analysing conflicts

a. Historical factors

During the workshop it was possible to look at the root causes of armed conflicts in eight countries. It became clear that the conflicts currently causing concern have their roots in a very varied range of trends and movements originating in the recent or distant past. Three key historical factors can be discerned which have had a near-universal impact, albeit one that has taken different forms in different regions of the world.

i. Colonial expansion

Colonial movements in the eighteenth, nineteenth and early twentieth centuries represented radical realignments in the control of the world's resources. Most of the world's current conflict spots have been colonised in the past, and many have seen multiple waves of colonisers. Sri Lanka's ethnic conflict originated in the political structures which were the legacy of the British colonial regime. The Philippines has been colonised at different times by Spain, Japan and America; Vietnam by France, China and America. Colonisation gives rise to the extraction of resources to power blocks outside the country, to the creation or strengthening of elites with the power to exclude others from access to the dwindling economic resources, and to the deepening of divisions between different population groups within the country.

ii. Superpower involvement during the Cold War period

During the Cold War, the United States, the Soviet Union and China pursued their strategic interests through the establishment of spheres of influence in weaker regions and countries, often fighting each other through the medium of more localised conflicts. Vietnam and Cambodia were focal points in this tripartite struggle, while Afghanistan and the Philippines were both, in different ways, used as theatres for proxy superpower wars. The Lebanese civil war has likewise been a focus for proxy conflicts waged by regional superpowers, as was also the case in Central America.

iii. The end of the Cold War

The collapse of the Soviet Union, bringing an end to the global rivalry between it and the US, has had a different impact in different regions. In several South and Central American countries, it has led to a rapprochement between internal factions, between whom rivalries and conflicts had often been promoted by the US. Such healing processes have been strengthened by renewed aid flows from the US, which is no longer prepared to have civil wars raging on its doorstep. In Africa, despite some moves towards internationally-brokered peace settlements, such as those in Namibia and Angola, the overall trend has been towards the destabilisation and decay of centralised states previously propped up by strategic aid. This has resulted in a descent into fragmentation in countries such as Somalia, Zaire and — again — Angola. Similar trends can be seen in some Asian countries such as Afghanistan. In Europe the downfall of communism has led to a collapse of the ideological divide between East and West; however, it has also given rise to the disastrous fragmentation of several Eastern states.

In contrast, the Western powers continue to have strong economic reasons for wishing to maintain their influence in South-East Asia. Hence, there is continued support for repressive governments from Western business and military interests. The support of the West for reconstruction in countries such as Vietnam, which are still recovering from past wars, may be tied to the introduction of Western-advocated political structures, and economic policies which open up new opportunities for Western interests.

b. Economic factors

The depletion and over-exploitation of natural and human resources is a major factor in the rise of violent conflict. There is a complex relationship between conflict, and economic and environmental resources. As previously viable modes of production become increasingly unstable because of factors including drought, soil depletion, and political restrictions, competition between different resource users increases, and conflict between them becomes a struggle for the very integrity and survival of the group. The conflict in Somalia, in common with numerous other African examples of 'green wars', can be seen in such a light. Similarly, the problem of land and the erosion of use rights over it lies at the heart of many violent struggles. As can be seen in Sri Lanka's case, expulsion from the land limits people's chances of a future return to economic viability, fuelling the fires of despair, and adding in turn to the cycle of violence. Competition over major water resources may also give rise to political tensions; for instance, the Nile and Jordan valleys are both areas where observers have warned of the possibility of violence.

While it is true that depletion of the environmental resource base is a powerful spur to the emergence of violent conflict, it should also be emphasised that many of the root causes of environmental decline are themselves political. Conflict itself degrades the environment, and indeed deliberate destruction of one's opponent's environmental resources has throughout history been used as a weapon of war. Methods employed range from the burning of farmland and the slaughtering of animals, to aerial bombing with napalm, as used by the US in Vietnam or Ethiopia in Eritrea.

The struggle for control of economic resources may involve intangible factors such as contacts and influence. These were major factors in conflicts in many Central and South American countries during the 1970s and 1980s. An example is El Salvador, which was dominated by an alliance between the government, the military, and the business elite, all of whom had strong international links. In the context of a huge economic gulf between the elite and the ordinary citizens, and a state ideology which brooked no dissenting voices, corruption and human rights violations resulted in protest which was violently suppressed. The subsequent emergence of a socialist liberation movement was viewed by the superpowers as justifying their provision of military aid and propaganda to combat what they saw as the 'enemy within'. Foreign investment increasingly shifted control of the country's resources away from the people. Many countries in South-East Asia, and in the Third World as a whole, show trends similar to those of Central America. In such economic inequities lie the seeds of conflict.

c. Political factors

Political ideologies play an important role in determining the degree to which a community or nation is able to maintain cohesion. Governments which retain a commitment towards equal representation of and sharing between different interest groups may be able to withstand the potentially divisive impact of structural poverty and environmental decline, as has been seen in the case of Tanzania. Many observers attribute the optimism which greeted the newly-created nation of Eritrea to the ideology of popular participation espoused by the leaders of the liberation struggle throughout the privations of the war years. Policies included actively encouraging women to take part in agriculture, politics, and the military struggle, and discouraging such factors as repressive marriage laws, which may inhibit women's full self-expression and participation.

On the other hand, where the driving force behind government actions is the need to maintain the status quo, the subjection of minorities and political opponents to repression and abuse is often unrestrained, until challenged by insurrection.

Unclear or changing ideologies may increase the risk of destabilisation, especially to governments trying to maintain cohesion in transitional periods. In Vietnam, for example, the current regime is trying on one hand to maintain unity between the northern and southern halves of the united country, and on the other to normalise relations with its former enemies and with other countries in the ASEAN region. Centralised political power has facilitated social and economic recovery and reconstruction, but has also led to opposition from those wishing to see a more individualistic economic regime. A move in 1988 towards a more open economy has only partially helped to defuse this opposition, and in addition has encouraged both capital outflow and political corruption, leading to a loss of confidence in the government.

d. Military factors

The economic and political factors described above have not only led to an increased incidence of conflict in the Third World. Allied to technological developments in modern warfare, these factors have also contributed to changes in the way wars are conducted. Armed conflict is becoming increasingly deregulated; its impact can no longer be contained within the bounds of formal armies and battlefields, but is played out in the homes, fields and forests of ordinary families and communities. Civilians provide marauding armies with resources ranging from food, transport, and information, to sexual favours.

The importance, in present-day conflicts, of sapping the enemy's morale, as opposed to merely destroying its military power, results in the use of food denial and environmental destruction, as weapons of war. Such practices have been often referred to in relation to Somalia, but are in fact a feature of conflict situations throughout the world. They are not confined to informal, internal conflicts but have also characterised a number of international wars during the latter half of the twentieth century, notably the US war in Vietnam and the US-led attacks on Iraq in the Gulf War. NGOs providing relief supplies may be caught up in the tendency of warring parties to use the withholding of food and other critical basic needs as weapons of war.

While the increasing desperation, impoverishment and cynicism, as well as the mobility, of armed forces promotes the increasing utilisation of ordinary men and women as providers of resources, more sinister still is their use as pawns in the strategic power games of their leaders. The most appalling example of this is the use of gender-specific violence as an attack on morale. Rape is employed as a means of degrading 'enemy' women, or women in occupied territory, and is currently being used extensively in Bosnia. Violence against men is exemplified in the phenomenon of 'disappearing' men in Central and South America.

Governments faced with incipient civil war which they aim to quell through repression have similarly developed the use of terror tactics. In the case of the Philippines, the government strategy for dealing with insurgency relies on provincial 'strike units' which operate secretly, unpredictably, and indiscriminately. Arbitrary arrests and killings are common, and community leaders, whatever their allegiance, are vulnerable. The strategy aims overtly to turn communities into battlefields. People living in communities affected in this way have no choice but to leave their homes, for their own protection. An estimated 200,000 internally displaced people in the Philippines, mostly women and children, have been obliged to move to controlled hamlets, living there under military supervision.

No account of the military factors affecting present-day conflict situations could be complete without reference to modern technological developments in armaments manufacture. These developments have facilitated the widespread marketing of weapons which are both reliably destructive and easy to use. There is nothing new about violence, nor is it necessarily always negative; some would argue that throughout human history it has played a role in regulating conflict and channelling social division. Modern weaponry, however, facilitates conflicts which, in the past, might have been kept within manageable bounds, to spill over into catastrophic destruction before mechanisms for reconciliation can come into play. Clan conflict in Somalia is a case in point. Many new types of weapon have been developed — for example, scatter-bombs, poison gas, chemical defoliants, and anti-personnel mines — which cause maximum civilian casualties. Some of these — such as anti-personnel mines — are very cheap to produce, and have been used in huge numbers. Mines have a catastrophic and far-reaching impact on civilians, resulting in thousands of deaths, injuries and permanent disabilities. In addition, they render farmland and water supplies unusable for years to come, unless de-mining projects can be completed.

e. How conflict affects communities

At community level, a pattern emerges of three different experiences of conflict. The first is characterised by the total destruction of the community's habitat: homes are destroyed, roads and bridges rendered impassable, water supplies cut off or polluted, constant attack on inhabitants obliges them to abandon their homes and move elsewhere. Affected communities, if they survive at all, are likely to become dependent on relief aid. As displaced people or as refugees, their members may be obliged to move several times, as their options for refuge become narrower. They face the prospect of never being able to return to their homes, living perpetually in temporary shelter or camps. Though many communities affected in this way try to keep together, in practice the United Nations estimates that 80 per cent of the refugees and displaced of the world are women and children whose menfolk have either left to fight, been killed in fighting, or, taking advantage of men's comparative mobility, have migrated to find better options elsewhere.

The second common conflict scenario is one in which the community's own habitat is not completely destroyed but is sufficiently disrupted to make continued existence there very difficult. The community's productive base is destroyed through lack of supplies, lack of access to land, or the destruction through looting of crops and animals. At regional or state level general instability and the breakdown of authority (sometimes triggered by external sanctions) leads to the collapse of commercial systems, including markets, money supply, and the provision of essential products and services, including the provision of health and education services, fuel and water supplies, and so on. Extreme shortages and raging inflation are likely to result.

Even if the community as a whole does not move, sections of it are likely to be obliged to go elsewhere in search of better options. Men may move in search of jobs, young people in search of education, and individuals may flee from persecution. Exceptionally, it may be women who choose to leave, as in the case of Filipina domestic workers migrating to the Gulf, or sex workers in the cities of South-East Asia.

The third common conflict scenario is one in which the community's territory is invaded or used as a base by armed groups. These may demand to be maintained by local people, who are forced to provide food, shelter, information, and transport, as in the case of Renamo in Mozambique or the Contras in Nicaragua. Men and boys may be forced to join the invaders, while women and girls are forced to provide sexual services. Terror tactics may be used to create divisions between different sections of the community, as has happened in contested regions of Somalia, or to ensure total submission to the invading movement, as in the case of Renamo in Mozambique. Similarly, liberation movements may, with the initial support and endorsement of elements within the community, inveigle themselves into villages and towns for the purpose of survival and subsistence. These communities will then become the focus of state military aggression and paramilitary violence.

To sum up, conflict affects communities by leading to the death, maiming or migration of individual community members. It affects the economic viability of the community by destroying its productive resource base, either in the short term (by, for example, destroying crops and animals), or in the long term (by denying access to land, or by destroying seed grain and local crop varieties). This may lead to gross impoverishment, to famine, or to flight and dependence on relief aid.

As will be discussed more fully in the next section, war also affects the psycho-social health and sense of identity of the community by promoting schisms and breaking up families, disrupting gender structures and relations, and by inflicting on individual members traumatic experiences which seriously impair their capacity to carry out their responsibilities. Adults who are themselves unable to cope with trauma are less able to ensure the recovery of their children who have lived through distressing experiences, thus perpetuating emotional ill-health into later generations. The ability of a community to protect the vulnerable, maintain social networks, and reduce the general stress of living for vulnerable members, is a key contributory factor in the ability of individuals to recover from trauma.

Given the complexity of the subject of armed conflict, analysing a typology of conflict is difficult. Moreover, such an exercise may seem to be of little help to the victims of conflict, for whom these distinctions may be purely academic. However, attempting an analysis of conflict may assist those working in conflict situations to understand the background and the contributory factors, and so shorten the time needed to make a relevant response.

f. Types of conflict

In attempting a synthesis of the causes and features of conflict discussed thus far, it may be helpful to draw a distinction between international conflicts and intra-state conflicts (see Figure 1). The distinction between international and internal conflict is significant for NGOs engaged in lobbying work. Most international attention and legal instruments have focused on conflicts between states. The limitations on the involvement of the international community in the 'internal affairs' of particular countries have yet to be defined satisfactorily.

International conflicts involve wars between states or the invasion of one state by another, as in the case of Vietnam and Cambodia. Conflict of this nature tends to be characterised as high-profile warfare between states, formally declared and involving organised armies. Highly trained soldiers use sophisticated weaponry whose impact they may never personally witness. The effect on ordinary civilians is extremely destructive and involves immobilisation of infra-structure (roads, bridges, factories, etc) as well as loss of life, a grossly polluted environment, and distorted political and social structures. A feature of such warfare (one that is still barely acknowledged) is the damage inflicted by warring states on their own soldiers.

Also included in the category of international conflict are proxy wars; these appear to be internal wars, which are in fact substantially fomented by states appearing to be external to the conflict operating through one of the warring parties. Examples of this can be seen in the cases of Afghanistan, Lebanon, and El Salvador.

In contrast, intra-state conflicts usually involve so-called 'low-intensity conflict', fuelled by internal tensions. In civil war, one or more parties oppose the state or vie for control of the state. These parties may be aiming for independence or autonomy for their own group or region, as in the case of East Timor or the Tamils in Sri Lanka. Alternatively, as in the case of the Burma opposition movements, they may seek the transformation of the whole of the state apparatus into one which they hope will respond more effectively to the needs of the population. Some countries, for example, South Africa, may experience this form of conflict as a reaction to the distortion of normal political and social relations by an ethnic or class minority. While most opposition groups take a principled stand or represent the voice of a particular marginalised group, others are the puppets of stronger states anxious to demonstrate the existence of an internal opposition in countries of an opposing block. The 'contra' movements in Central America and Renamo in Mozambique are examples of such puppet opposition groups.

Intra-state conflict may also result from the fragmentation which accompanies the collapse of states, as in regions of Eastern Europe and in Somalia. It also includes situations of generalised repression and 'hidden' civil war, which may be a precursor of full-scale civil war. In intra-state conflict, violence is not confined to theatres of war, and may not be limited to formal military operations. The distinction between armed forces and civilians is blurred by the tendency of fighters towards informal organisation. These fighters may wear no uniform and have no special accommodation. Commanders may be unable or unwilling to exercise discipline over loose bands of desperate supporters, or ensure a common understanding of policy among officials operating far from decision-making centres. Ordinary members of the public may willingly or unwillingly take part in the conflict in different ways — taking messages, taking part in demonstrations, throwing stones, etc.

At this point, it should be emphasised that the distinction between different types of conflict cannot be pushed too far. The Gulf War illustrates the way in which inter- and intra-state conflict can combine and reinforce each other in practice. The Gulf War, a classic example of a high profile international conflict, was also linked inextricably with other internal and regional conflicts. Despite its limitations, however, the distinction may be useful in clarifying thinking about the factors involved, if only to emphasise the need for a more coherent typology of conflict to be developed.

Fig. 1 Types of conflict

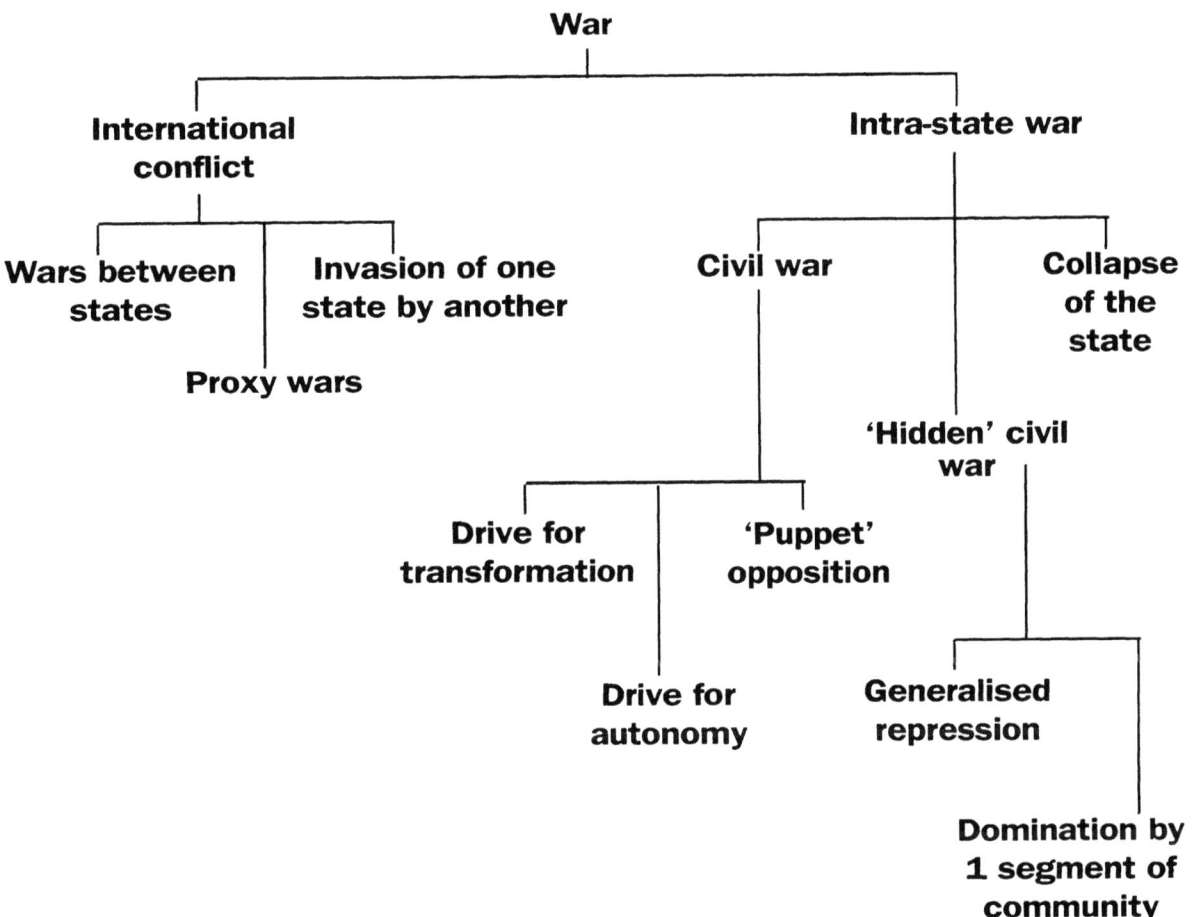

Judy el Bushra, ACORD

Fig. 2 Conflict as a process

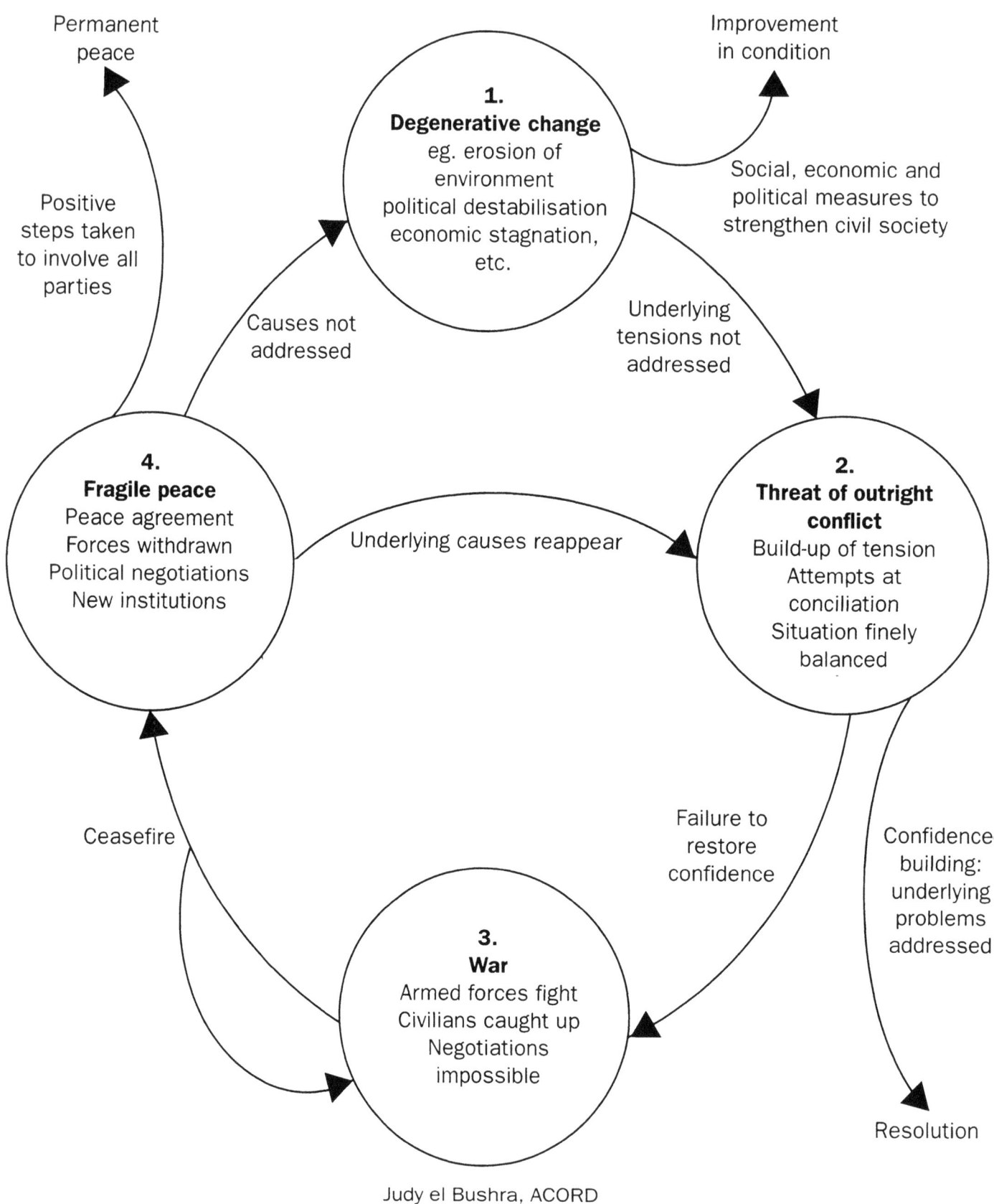

Judy el Bushra, ACORD

Key Concepts:
Critical thresholds: critical moments when a situation is poised to move in either a positive or negative direction, and when it is susceptible to influence.

Stabilising points: elements within a situation (e.g. people, physical resources, institutions etc.) which tend towards stability.

1.3 Conflict as a process

We have seen that conflict always has a past: its roots may be set in old rivalries, long-standing degeneration in living standards, or thwarted political aspirations. It takes many forms and involves complex linkages between a variety of factors. Conflict changes the environment in which it occurs. It is a process which evolves over time in response to a shifting kaleidoscope of underlying factors, which are, in turn, changed by it.

Conflict also changes the options available to individuals and communities caught up in these conflicts, either restricting them or sometimes broadening them. It can deepen the poverty and vulnerability from which it grew, or, in other instances, can challenge the past and open up new avenues to allow people the chance of positive reconstruction.

While no two conflicts are the same, there remain some common patterns which can help us to understand the dynamics of particular conflicts, anticipate their likely outcome, and decide upon appropriate action.

Figure 2 presents a theoretical model for the way in which conflict occurs. According to this model, conflict finds its roots in degenerative change which, if unchecked, can leave a community vulnerable to events that can bring it to the brink of conflict. If appropriate measures are not taken, outright war may result, from which recovery and eventual peace is possible under the right conditions.

It should be noted that this model does not aim to portray conflict as a linear process which must necessarily pass through certain predetermined stages. Rather, it illustrates how particular points in the evolution of a conflict may form 'critical thresholds' at which alternative options present themselves. These can lead either to a peaceful outcome or to a spiral of descent into turbulence and war.

Underlying causes of unrest must, therefore, be acknowledged and dealt with, rather than ignored or suppressed. In particular, processes of democratisation and popular self-expression must be promoted by the encouragement of a dynamic and self-confident civil society, to form the main 'stabilising point' around which new consensus may be built.

The development of a representative, popular civil society must include the open and frank discussion of gender relations and the need to facilitate the full social and political participation of women. Gender relations are integral to all societies and are, as such, a factor in social change or stasis.

1.4 A new model of development

The above analysis points the way to a view of the development process which takes into account the critical linkages between conflict and the factors which underlie it, seeing conflict as both a symptom and a cause of processes of impoverishment. In addition, it acknowledges the role NGOs can play in influencing — positively or negatively — the outcome of violent situations.

External influences at the point of a 'critical threshold' are frequently significant in tipping the balance to one side or another; hence, the decisions of NGOs as to where to place their support can count strongly towards determining a positive outcome and ensuring peace and stability. In this sense their 'neutrality' is illusory.

Following this, if development agencies are to respond adequately to the challenges raised by armed conflict, they must now question and reinterpret some of the basic assumptions which have guided their work in the past. The volatile conditions under which most development NGOs now work call into question the assumption that development is a gentle progression along a path of normality. Crisis has now become the normality in many areas of the world, and development a process of adaptation to crisis.

A number of conclusions can be drawn from this. First, despite the speed of change and the apparent randomness with which it occurs, stable patterns can be detected in the dynamics of pre-conflict and conflict situations which, as we have seen above, can help to predict possible outcomes or lend weight to positive changes, which may avoid conflict. Where conflict seems inevitable, recognising such patterns can help those concerned to prepare for the worst scenarios. To identify these patterns we need to be-aware of the complexity of social change, and of the reverberating waves of change that can be triggered off by seemingly minor, distant, or unconnected events.

Secondly, the dichotomy between development and emergency work is no longer useful, grounded in linear, evolutionist views of development which do not reflect the multiple realities of the situations in which NGOs work. Poor and marginalised communities need to be able to cope with emergencies if they are to survive in the long term; yet the way in which they cope with the emergencies may determine the quality of their survival in the future.[4] From the point of view of NGO operations, the same paradox applies. It is not possible to ignore the short-term survival needs of populations they work with, yet how they attempt to address them may be critical for long-term recovery. **Emergency interventions must serve the long-term development goals of strengthening the community's own capacity to deal with rapid and turbulent change**.

With this in mind, short-term work in conflict situations should be based on the basic principles of all high-quality development work. NGOs should take the time to listen to the people who are on the scene (and that means women, as well as men), and to think through the consequences of their actions as outsiders; to think broadly and without preconceptions about a range of possible types of support; and to continually revise, and try to refine, their understanding of the social reality in which they are involved.

Thirdly, NGOs need to reconsider not only the development concepts and theoretical planning tools that they use, but also the way in which they themselves are structured and managed. **Working in conflict requires a flexible and rapid response and a minimum of bureaucracy.** It also requires that centralised decision-making processes should give way to the deployment of relatively independent teams of front-line workers — well-trained women and men, confident and empowered to take initiatives as necessary.

Lastly, it is critically important for planners in conflict situations to focus on processes of social differentiation. As we have said, conflict takes place in the context of pre-existing patterns of social differentiation and has, in turn, its own impact on them. The natural partners of NGOs are the poorest, the oppressed and the vulnerable — but, even within those categories, there are divisions and conflicting interests. Under the pressure of urgency (in many cases exacerbated by the assumptions and *modus operandi* of NGOs), researching the micro level may seem to cause unnecessary delay. However, if NGOs operate without doing so, their support may misfire and runs the risk of marginalising the very groups who are most acutely in need of help.

Gender issues clearly figure largely here. Section 2 gives a conceptual and practical account of how conflict analysis can be enriched through an awareness of such social differentiation. As we shall see, looking at conflict through the eyes of women changes our view of conflict as well as our relationship with communities affected by conflict, enabling us to react more sensitively to the economic, political and military complexities of war, while giving us a more holistic view of conflict as a dynamic force.

I.2 The Gender Dimensions of Armed Conflict

Section I 2 describes the impact of conflict on women and on gender relations using different levels of analysis

A training session for health workers on how to help women and men traumatised by violence, Uganda

2 THE GENDER DIMENSIONS OF ARMED CONFLICT

2.1 Introduction

This section has two parts. The first of these synthesises the preceding discussion of conflict with the reality of women's experiences in conflict situations. This reality amplifies and refines our understanding of the complexities of conflict. The second part draws some conclusions about the impact of armed conflict on gender relations and makes explicit some of the theoretical and analytical links between gender and conflict.

We will look in particular at how women are negatively affected by conflict and turbulent change. This part of the paper will focus on women's vulnerability, and how changes in their situation lead, in many cases, to lower status, increased marginalisation, and perhaps to greater abuse of their human rights.

However, we need to start by challenging the common wisdom of many development practitioners, who see women and their children as vulnerable and assume this vulnerability is natural. We believe that women are made vulnerable by the complex web of discriminatory practices and male-oriented institutions in society. From unequal feeding practices which discriminate against girls in early childhood, to the many examples of behavioural restrictions in adulthood, women are made to conform to cultural norms which often restrict them from developing to their full physical, mental and spiritual potential.

The gender analysis of development has tended towards two main approaches. The first looks at gender from a broadly economic perspective, seeing the issue of differential access to and control over resources as the critical factor in social processes. When looking at conflict this approach extends our understanding of poverty and vulnerability in war by emphasising the different impact conflict has on the economic stability and survival strategies of women and of men.

In contrast, the second approach to gender analysis tends to centre on issues of women's needs and status ('condition' and 'position'), and subsumes debates about poverty and disempowerment in this political analysis. This approach recognises that women of poor Third World countries have been consistently marginalised in relation to structures of power in the political, military, and media arenas, and emphasises women's need for a space to voice their needs and concerns. This approach can be useful in examining ways to support women's efforts to retain or claim such a space during conflict, and highlights how conflict adversely affects women's already marginalised position within society.

Oxfam's belief is that these two approaches occupy much common ground and each has important insights to offer. This report aims to combine the two by highlighting empirical evidence of women's coping strategies in conflict situations, as well as the theoretical issues of women's status within their society which feminist analysis indicates are critical for women. Yet it aims to do so while recognising the reality of most women's lives as deeply intertwined with those of the families and communities in which they live.

2.2 Women's experience of conflict

This section draws on the case studies (given in Part II), and the debates and discussions that took place at the workshop, to consider the ways in which conflict changes women's lives: as individuals (the personal sphere), as members of the family or household (the private sphere) and as members of the community (the public sphere).

In reality, of course, women experience conflict in a holistic way; however, drawing a distinction between these three spheres may nevertheless be useful as a conceptual framework for analysis.

a. The personal sphere

i. The risks and consequences of personal danger

Armed conflict involves everyone, not just armed protagonists, in the risk of increased violence. The risk of direct or accidental attack affects individuals as they go about their daily business. It is difficult for women to avoid this danger. Whether working in their fields or searching for food, water or fuel, selling produce by the roadside, or taking part in community activities, they risk being attacked, blown up by land mines or caught in crossfire. Mobility may be a key factor in personal survival. Women may not be able to run away with the same ease as men, encumbered perhaps by pregnancy or by the need to watch over children, the sick and the old.

Beyond this, women are particularly vulnerable to sexual violence and rape. Rape is obviously not something that arises only in conflict situations; rape and the threat of rape are part of daily life for women the world over, whether they are conscious of it or not. In non-conflict situations, rape and other forms of violence against women represent a horrifying catalogue of abuse, with huge social as well as personal costs.[5] Women who never experience such violence are nevertheless socialised from an early age into an awareness of rape and violence as a threat both to their persons and to their — and their family's — honour.

Conflict increases women's vulnerability while simultaneously strengthening those social, cultural and personal factors which lead men to rape. First, fear of violence and rape limits women's ability to go to market, work in fields, stand in queues for food aid, look for firewood, and so on. Personal danger has consequences for women's mobility, an important component of their economic functions. As providers of food and shelter for their families (a role which is likely to be expanded in the absence of men) they will need to be more hard-working, more resourceful, and to take even more physical risks to meet their family's needs. Women in Cambodia, for example (see case study), had to retrace their steps back to the villages they had fled from under bombardment, in order to collect their harvests from their fields.

Recent publicity in the international media has highlighted the use of rape as a weapon in intercommunal violence in the former Yugoslavia, with soldiers being exhorted to rape and kill women as part of the war effort. Estimates of the number of women raped vary between

50 — 80,000.[6] Though this may appear to be an extreme example, the cases presented in this report suggest that rape may be routine in conflict situations, perpetrated by troops who may have the encouragement of their commanders. Burma, the Philippines and Uganda are just a few of the countries where the number of women and girls raped by soldiers runs into thousands.

Women may have great difficulty in speaking up about their experiences and hence in getting practical help and counselling. As the Burma case study shows, women do not feel able to talk about their experiences of rape. Beyond that, the experience of rape invariably has dire long-term consequences for women.[7] Many women become dishonoured in the eyes of their community, and suffer a loss of self-esteem. In these cases, ostracised from society, prostitution may become the only way to survive. In certain Muslim areas in the south of the Philippines, for instance, prostitution was unknown until government troops moved into the area to put down the secessionist movement of the 1970s, raping thousands of women and committing other atrocities.

So prevalent is the incidence of rape and other forms of sexual harassment against women in times of conflict, that many women accept sexual alliances with soldiers or other men in positions of power as a means of protection, escape or simple survival. This strategy is a particularly important one in the case of young women, as for example in Northern Uganda, where some mothers have adopted the tactic of marrying their daughters to soldiers at puberty in order to limit the risk of rape.[8] Reports from Mozambique describe the virtual enslavement of young boys and girls in Renamo camps, where boys, who are themselves traumatised by violence, frequently inflict violent sexual acts upon the girls.[9] Girls may be obliged to suffer these in order to avoid being killed or starved.

It is also necessary to note the existence of male rape, as a phenomenon which is more widespread in both peace-time and in conflict than is readily acknowledged. Its existence adds weight to the interpretation of rape as an exercise in power, domination, and humiliation, rather than a purely sexual act. Though male rape may be less extensive than rape of women, its impact on the individual concerned may be more destructive, because it may be even more difficult to discuss openly.

There is some evidence that certain types of conflict increase levels of domestic violence against women. Apartheid, and other regimes which exercise power by undermining people's self-esteem and self-expression, encourage and strengthen relationships of domination on gender lines as well as class and ethnic lines. Certainly, very high incidence of rape and domestic violence are reported in South Africa.

ii. Health and disability

Good health is critical to women's ability to cope with their many responsibilities. Women's health issues on which conflict may have an impact include psychological and reproductive health as well as general health and issues concerning women's access to food and community support.

Conflict reduces the standards of living and levels of resource availability in society as a whole, and destroys health, welfare and education services. Women are doubly vulnerable to this reduction in resources and support. First, physical vulnerability is higher than that of men due to women's sexual and reproductive role. Extensive rape as a constituent of conflict may give rise to the spread of sexually transmitted diseases, including AIDS, and to untold numbers of unwanted pregnancies (see Uganda case study). Complications of pregnancy and childbirth may remain untreated in the absence of medical services. Women may also be more vulnerable than men to a reduction in resources; this socially-rooted vulnerability is seen in communities where men have preferential rights to command the resources of the community. For example, in societies where women are the last to eat, they are invariably the first to suffer from famine.

The patterns and characteristics of psychological stress and trauma resulting from conflict are not yet properly understood. Trauma is defined as a 'psychological state resulting from an extreme experience'.[10] Possible causes of trauma in conflict situations include the following:

- physical privation, injury, torture
- imprisonment and or sustained threat of death
- witnessing torture or massacres
- violent or humiliating death of loved ones
- rape
- destitution, loss of home, property, livelihood
- destruction of one's community
- forced migration.

Post-traumatic stress disorder (PTSD) is the term used for a cluster of symptoms, including depression, suicide, increased incidence of various forms of mental illness, fatigue, listlessness, recurrent recollection of traumatic events, startling easily, and explosive anger. Reactions to post-traumatic stress tend to form a sequence in which initial shock is followed by efforts to cope with and manage the situation. This critical phase is strongly influenced by a person's circumstances. Additional stress factors, such as the need to struggle to find food, have a negative effect on the person's ability to cope; feelings of being out of control or of having lost the capacity for personal choice are additional stress factors. The inability to cope with trauma may result in mental illness. On the other hand, recovery can be helped by positive factors, such as good social networks. Given the support of a close-knit community, individuals who experience such trust and encouragement have often shown themselves to be highly resilient in the face of trauma induced by conflict, violence, abuse, and torture.

Gender-sensitive studies carried out in refugee communities in Mozambique, Zambia and Central America have pointed to differences between men and women in the way people deal with trauma.[11] Whereas women tended to worry most about family issues, such as their relationships with their children and husband, men were more likely to worry about factors outside the family, such as the lack of access to facilities. This can be explained by the construction of gender roles and identities, whereby women are socialised since early childhood into caring roles, with the family as the primary focus. In these studies, women tended to show greater feelings of helplessness than men; In addition, they appeared to have less access to social support networks beyond the family, as well as less time to make use of those that existed. Single women or women who have lost their families or other social support may be most at risk. However, it should be noted that, in some cases, far from providing a support, the marriage relationship may be a source of additional stress for women.

The inability of parents, and particularly mothers, to deal with their own stress can impair the ability of traumatised boys and girls to come to terms with their experiences. Women may actually react to stress by withdrawal from their children. In addressing the problems of traumatised children, it is therefore paramount to provide support for their carers.

Some experiences of providing support to traumatised people indicate the need for the provision of a 'safe space' where people take refuge from the daily struggle for survival to work through their feelings in an unpressurised, therapeutic manner.[12] Such a space offers people the opportunity to share their experiences and hence to give them meaning and value. In other situations, such as that described in the Sri Lanka case study, it seems important to offer women the opportunity to take active roles in rehabilitation programmes, as a medium- to long-term means of overcoming post-traumatic stress.

Trauma resulting from extreme violence may also have the effect of conditioning those who experience it to accept violent behaviour as normal. Men who in warfare have been obliged to torture, rape, and kill may find reintegration into normal society and into their families difficult. As a result, some men may be conditioned by their experiences to inflict violence against others without provocation.[13] Their victims are often their own wives and female relatives.

Men traumatised in this way may find social relationships difficult to sustain; they may find it hard to determine a satisfactory role for themselves in households which may have survived for some time without them. The reintegration of men into their families and communities is an important element in the reconstruction process, which can be worked through together with women. This will bring benefits for the community as a whole.

Disability is another consequence of war where the gender aspects need further investigation. In Somaliland, where thousands of land mines were left behind by ex-President Siad Barre's retreating army, the majority of people who lose limbs from land mine or other accidents are women and children gathering fuel, collecting water or attempting to cultivate the land. With few prostheses available, disabled women find it difficult to carry out productive activities and tasks in the home. The Cambodia case study shows how a spouse's reaction to a partner's disability is differentiated by sex: whereas a wife's disablement is a common contribution to marital breakdown, disabled husbands have every expectation that their wives will stay with them and shoulder the added burden of responsibility.

iii. Personal identity and self-esteem

Self-esteem and the sense of personal identity which is linked to this are complex feelings, incorporating elements of personal psychology as well as culturally-determined values. Female identity, varying across cultures, is affected in conflict situations in different ways. Violence and brutality, changes in gender roles, and in family status, all demand a high degree of energy from women to ensure their own mental stability and emotional survival. Many women may also have to find the strength to live on in an altered family structure if they are widowed or abandoned.

A non-threatening and accepting environment is vital to promoting personal self-esteem and reaffirming identity. This is one in which women can survive with their families in the way they find most appropriate to their altered circumstances, without pressure to conform to prevailing values and practices.

An environment which marginalises women or singles them out as violating societal norms can render them outcasts, in their own eyes as well as those of others. For many women, personal identity is tied closely to issues of sexuality, marriage, and family. Rape is therefore experienced not only a personal and social attack, but also as an act of defilement which strikes deep into a woman's sense of her own worth and her concept of herself as a woman. In societies which focus solely on women as wives and mothers, loss of, or separation from, her husband or children may signify for a woman a loss of identity and status, adding to the emotional strain caused by the loss of the loved one.

Women who do not marry or bear children, because of the demographic imbalance caused by war, may suffer a similar sense of lost womanhood. Reports from Vietnam and Cambodia describe how some women of the war generation, finding themselves nearing menopause alone, seek out informal sexual relationships with men on the grounds that to be left without children is a worse fate than suffering the disapproval of society.

Women's sense of identity may also include adherence to culturally-defined gender norms of correct behaviour. In many cultures, female identity and self-esteem is reflected outwardly in standards of modest dress and scrupulous personal hygiene. These standards may be difficult or impossible to maintain in times of conflict. In Somalia, many women lost their clothes, which meant that they could not leave their homes to receive food aid. The provision of culturally acceptable clothing as part of relief projects may, in a case like this, be valued as highly as food and shelter. Similarly, some emergency projects are now starting to send items of personal hygiene, such as soap, sanitary towels and underwear, in relief packages, in an acceptance of the fact that maintaining self-respect is as important for mental well-being as food and dwellings are for physical survival.

Undefinable feelings of loss of identity and value may inhibit women's recovery from trauma, and prevent them from exercising their rights as individuals and members of society. In contrast, social disruption caused by conflict and its aftermath may allow previously unquestioned assumptions about gender norms to be challenged. This may lead to changes in the way women perceive and value their roles, and an awareness of alternative visions.

It is significant that it is in societies where women have taken an active role in socio-political struggles (perhaps in independence, liberation or feminist movements) that there has been a marked and positive redefinition and affirmation of women's identity. Women's active participation in struggles for political and social self-determination seems critically important in forming new role models and challenging previous gender stereotypes in positive ways.[14]

The Central American case study points out that, after two decades of war, there is now a greater awareness of women taking on non-traditional roles. Although it is true that Christian fundamentalism is pushing women back home to be mothers and wives, communities have had to come to terms more than ever with single mothers, female-headed households, female guerrilla fighters, and popular resistance leaders, who unite their communities while confronting institutionalised repression. Each one of these roles represents new possibilities for changing oppressive gender ideologies.

What has not yet taken place is a significant parallel redefinition of male identities. Perhaps only a revolution in the sexual division of labour can provide a real possibility for such a radical change in gender roles and the cultural constructions of masculinity and femininity.

b. The private sphere

For the majority of women, the family is likely to be their principal arena of responsibility. Women may thus define themselves chiefly in relationship to family members, as mother and wife. Conflict places the integrity of the family in question. Husbands, fathers and sons may leave to join armies, may be killed, disabled, or abducted. Women may be forced to take part in the fighting or to provide sexual or other services for the combatants. Family members may lose each other during flight, and marriage partners may suffer divided allegiances, and part.

Though women's own suffering may affect the way they are able to carry out their own roles within the family, the suffering of other family members also has an impact on women. These crises are lived through at a time when the community's and the family's material and social resources are already stretched. Their net result is to place on women an increased burden of providing, both economically and emotionally; and at the same time, cause a drastic reduction in the degree of support available to help them to do this with no immediate prospect of change in their position.

i. Changes in women's economic roles

Conflict often destroys or damages the ways in which a family earns money or feeds itself. Farming may no longer be viable if there is insufficient labour available, if seed stocks have been eaten, or if produce is looted. Transport and marketing systems, providing marketing outlets and essential supplies, may have been destroyed. Those who are obliged to seek refuge away from home lose access to their land and perhaps their animals, and as refugees they may have few opportunities to earn a living.

In situations of economic crisis or decline due to conflict, both men and women find themselves shouldering increased burdens in meeting their obligations towards their families. However, these burdens may be heavier and more stressful for women, since crisis creates pressures on the family, which is the main focus of women's attention. The most difficult burdens are shouldered by women who are heads of households, among whom there are many women who are the sole adult provider. The proportion of female-headed households among refugee and displaced groups is very high: 25-50 per cent is not unusual, and it may be even higher.

The disadvantages faced by female-headed households are wide-ranging; the most obvious is the reduction in available adult labour and income-earning power. Linked to this is the problem of access to resources. Even in peacetime, women on their own without a man to speak on their behalf may have difficulty in legitimising their claims to land, or in obtaining credit. Community structures providing economic support are often restricted to men, and where this is not the case, women may have only passive roles within them. Thus, though women who head households have increased economic responsibilities, they do not have the increased access to and control over economic resources which is necessary for them to meet their obligations.

Women heads of households must therefore meet their own basic needs and those of their dependants in whatever way they can. This may mean adopting emergency survival mechanisms, for which these women are ill-equipped or untrained, or which in normal times would be considered socially unacceptable. The approval of one's community in such circumstances becomes an economic asset in itself, in that it enables the poorer to make claims on the support of their neighbours. Women in particular have to balance the economic advantages of engaging in possibly unacceptable activities against the support they are likely to receive from others if they conform to cultural mores.

Survival mechanisms in times of crisis fall into four main categories. These categories are in increasing order of severity and may follow in sequence as the crisis deepens. At the first stage, family providers try to make adaptations to their existing roles and within their existing environment. They will 'make do' by cooking cheaper foods, cutting down the number of meals eaten per day, reducing portions, or substituting home-made foods and remedies for bought ones. Many women go without food themselves in order to feed their families.

Resources may be exploited more exhaustively than usual, but this is effective only as long as the resources exist. However carefully the stored grain is eked out, if the crisis continues beyond a certain time, it will come to an end. 'Making do' is therefore only a good strategy if it enables gaps to be bridged until normality returns.

Such economising is likely to precede selling off assets: women heads of households may decide to liquefy their assets to buy food, selling jewellery or land and slaughtering animals. Decisions of this kind require judicious balancing of short- and long-term options, based on an intimate knowledge of the local environment. They are likely to be rational, even though they may not follow a logic familiar to outsiders. As might be expected, those assets of long-term utility are likely to go last.

Women who have not previously worked for payment may begin to do so. Women's informal sector activities often involve the turning of skills normally practised within the home to commercial advantage; income-generating activities may include selling food, tailoring, farm labour, domestic service or low-paid service jobs with the military.

Farmers of both sexes may switch to planting short-cycle crops, crops that can be stored in the ground until needed, crops that are rich in carbohydrates, or crops that can be grown close to the house, if the situation is very insecure. Farmers may have extensive knowledge of crops suitable for such circumstances, and may keep aside seed for unusual eventualities. One of the longer-term consequences of conflict is the loss of crop varieties specially adapted to local conditions; this is particularly significant in the case of crops cultivated by women, since they are often responsible for traditional varieties involving little cash or technological input, which are used for subsistence.

A second group of survival mechanisms come into operation when women are forced by death or desertion to take over tasks previously carried out by men. The Cambodia case study illustrates clearly some of the new roles women have had to adopt in the absence of men. In El Quiche, Guatemala, women carry out male farming tasks such as land-clearance and ploughing.[15] Women may take part in labour-intensive construction activities under food-for-work schemes. The intensity of women's new workload may, in some exceptional cases, lead to the remaining men taking over some of women's tasks, as has happened recently in some parts of Somalia, when men started helping women with the carrying of water and firewood. However, this is exceptional and is only likely to happen when men become aware of a commercial potential to the activity.

A third strategy is migration, either to places of refuge, to cities, or to other states, where opportunities include domestic work and petty trading. Where individuals or sections of a community migrate with the intention of seeking an income or better opportunities, they may or may not be able to send money home, but there is a strong likelihood that their links with their home and family will be maintained. In cases where whole families or communities have to abandon their homes, they may lose these permanently, and consequently undertake such a step only in cases of dire necessity. They may retain the hope of returning, and pass on the knowledge of their old home, for generations.

Fourthly, in extreme situations, women will take up activities which are not only new but may be socially unacceptable, or unacceptable in normal conditions. In some cultures which discourage women from working outside the home, petty commerce may be seen as acceptable for women who have no other choice. Selling drugs and alcohol may be acceptable activities in some societies but not in others. Other roles may be so badly regarded that women who take them on risk being completely rejected by their family and friends. Prostitution and other activities within the entertainment and sex tourism industries, such as dancing for troops and working in bars, normally fall within this group, as does black marketeering. Forming liaisons with enemy soldiers is the most ill-regarded action of all, and women may never regain their family's support or good opinion.

The factors which push women into taking on socially unacceptable roles are complex and inadequately understood. They include economic factors, such as the lack of other viable options for making a living; but economics alone does not explain why women take such steps, which often violate their self-respect as well as risking the complete breakdown of supportive relationships with family and community. The political complexities which underlie women's decision to take part in 'antisocial' activities, as exemplified in the prostitution industry which surrounded the US bases in the Philippines, also need to be better understood and linked to the personal issues.

ii. Changes to the sexual division of labour

The changes to women's economic role brought about by conflict may continue after hostilities cease. At best, the systemic shock caused by conflict can also provide opportunities for women to challenge and question their subordinate status, if change in the sexual division of labour is accompanied by a process of role integration and redefinition of individual and social identities. Women may learn new economic skills as a result of crisis, which they can later build on to gain confidence and respect. Previous stereotypes about what is or is not 'women's work' can be reconsidered, thus opening up new avenues for women. Significant advances in women's position have often taken place when a community faces the crisis of war or famine.

Crisis can thus empower women, though there is a danger that they will slip back again to their former positions if the community and the state do not fully understand the implications of the changes taking place, and provide the framework for them to be sustained. If men do not also adjust their roles, or reintegrate poorly into the post-conflict situation, there is a danger that the additional burden on women may simply result in overwork becoming institutionalised. The Uganda case study shows how, nearly a decade on, the war is perceived as one of the major factors leading to the enormously heavy workload women now shoulder, which is fast becoming a national calamity. A sexual division of labour which was previously quite rigid is now much more flexible, since returning menfolk have not necessarily returned to their old roles. Rather, men have tended to allow women to continue to take responsibility for essential household provisioning, and women have often been 'proud' to do so. This changing situation is creating problems of readjustment for men as well as women, and leading to problems of family breakdown and social dislocation due to the uncertainty over gender roles.

In order for a community to arrive at a proper understanding of the process of change to the sexual division of labour and women's economic role brought about by conflict, time and space for reflection are needed. In addition, the development of a confident women's movement answers the demand for support from women in new economic and social roles, and may affect the pace of social change. These considerations could form important areas of potential involvement for NGOs working in recovery and reconstruction.

iii. Demographic changes

The absence of men and increase in proportion of female-headed households are changes in household structure that may take place as a result of conflict. In time, conflict may result in a demographic imbalance, with short- and long-term consequences for patterns of marriage and household labour arrangements. As the Cambodia case study describes, such demographic imbalance has several negative consequences for women. Their 'value' in the marriage market is reduced, and they have little choice of marriage partner. Many women have a choice between accepting junior status as a second or third wife or not getting married at all, and may have to continue in unhappy or violent marriages for similar reasons. Educated and economically-independent women find themselves 'on the shelf' if they are seen as being insufficiently compliant.

As in Uganda, the stigma of the unmarried state and the difficulties of coping economically are serious disincentives to women living alone. Conversely, however, war sometimes encourages women to rely less on marriage as a means of support. The experience of having survived war with little help from men may make women reluctant to support husbands who do not contribute to the household, and less willing to bow to social pressure against divorce.

c. The public sphere

It is in this sphere that the range of macro and micro issues concerning women in conflict fuse to find concrete expression in gender-blind or overtly gender-oppressive structures and actions. For example, the deep-seated cultural concept of women as passive, vulnerable, and in need of male protection may find political expression in the violent sexual exploitation of women as a strategy for weakening the enemy's resistance. In reconstruction after conflict, the same reductive gender ideology may mean women have restricted or no access to communal economic and political resources which are critical for recovery. However, it is also in the public sphere that much of the potential for positive transformation of women's status lies.

i. Community structures

Women may potentially be able to seek protection or support from existing community mechanisms, including community organisations such as village committees and associations. However, experience shows that even where such mechanisms exist, (and they may be severely impaired in or after conflict), they do not always respond to women's needs since, in most communities, existing structures reflect patriarchal values and formations. In Somalia and Somaliland, for example, the existence of elders' committees has been an important factor in keeping communities together during wartime. However, there is little evidence that elders' committees have been able or willing to provide women with the opportunity to express their particular needs, given their exclusively male membership and their generally protectionist and stereotyped approach to women's needs.

Men may be reluctant to share vital economic resources in times of crisis, and may demand that benefits accruing to the community, such as food aid, are channelled to the family through them, rather than being distributed to all adults within the household. Women's needs are thus concealed and, in the pressure of emergency situations, are rarely deliberately sought out. This state of affairs also frequently applies in post-emergency recovery periods, and affects the distribution of emergency rations. As we have seen, conflict may allow configurations of power and control of resources to be redefined in ever-tighter and more irrevocable fashion; such channelling of resources through men may confirm women's subordinate status and help to perpetuate this on a permanent basis.

ii. Women and human rights issues

During a time of conflict, the idealised role of women as guardians of honour and cultural identity is critical as a means of regaining social cohesion. In societies undergoing stress or forced change, dominant groups or sectors may push towards and promote the suspension of women's human rights as a reaction to pressure from outside forces. In Somalia, the de facto military authorities have announced — and implemented — laws bringing in the death penalty for women suspected of mixing too freely with foreign soldiers.[16] Female refugees from Afghanistan found, in their Pakistani refugee camps, that they were expected to conform to much more stringent rules of dress than previously. A group's sense of honour and integrity is made manifest through the behaviour of women, and men's patriarchal capacity to control them.

The use of rape and other forms of violence against women as a strategy in war has already been discussed. However, it should be noted this human rights abuse is not only perpetrated by warring factions but may also be used as a strategy by the state military and paramilitary. An example is the abuse committed against women by government soldiers in Burma. In most cases the state apparatus condones or turns a blind eye towards this institutionalised gender violence, in repudiation of its responsibility to work for the protection of all citizens, set high standards of behaviour among its own staff, and permit open examination of complaints of human rights abuse.

The lack of protection for women and lack of respect for their human rights observed on the ground during war situations has not been seriously or effectively challenged by the international community. The failure to uphold women's human rights in wartime extends beyond those who have a direct interest in the outcome of a war to a variety of bodies with the capacity to influence opinion. For example, despite the provisions of the 1949 Geneva Convention outlawing attacks on civilians, and despite much lobbying from Northern women's groups, the United Nations has so far failed to take up the challenge of condemning the atrocities in Bosnia in concrete terms. While the UN has recognised the need to address the issue of rape in the context of war crimes, no women have been appointed to investigation panels and the issue is generally regarded as 'difficult'.

Other authorities have similarly failed to condemn outright the sexual abuse of women in Bosnia. The Pope, promoting the image of women as passive recipients of whatever injustice comes their way, has publicly urged women who have become pregnant as a result of rape to 'accept the enemy' by welcoming the children they have conceived, rather than seeking abortion.[17] The Imam of Zagreb expressed a more positive opinion: 'We need to change our mentality when confronted by these women and cannot consider them in the light of our ancient customs'.[18]

The validity of women's image of vulnerability is central to gender and conflict issues. In most societies, women do not engage in warfare since they are viewed as in need of protection. The shielding of women, children, the sick and old in times of emergency is given a high value. This idealised picture, however, does not necessarily correspond to the reality. In Somalia for example, where protecting the wives and children of one's enemies is a point of honour in warfare, this code has been maintained by individuals. However, it has been broken on a wider scale, through numerous examples of massacres of women and children. What are the circumstances under which these rules of engagement break down? Why have such atrocities occurred in Somalia, but almost never in neighbouring Eritrea, where standards of conduct among the troops of the liberation movements were very high? The issue here is to recognise that, parallel to the ideology of women as vulnerable and in need of defence, exists the reality of violence against women as a permanent feature of many societies. This violence, which is normally found within the family, may be brought into the public sphere in situations of conflict.

As was highlighted at the UN Conference on Human Rights, the present state of protection and promotion of women's human rights is abysmal. 'Much of what women experience as everyday abuse in their lives ... is still seen as largely outside the terrain of the human rights community.'[19] This includes significant human rights abuses in situations of conflict. Although the definition of rape as a war crime represents a new awareness, the attention of humanitarian and human rights organisations needs to focus on the varied forms of gender-based violence in conflict, and measures to combat these should be enacted. In particular, there is a need to look at sexual violence — ranging from harassment to gang rape — experienced by refugee and displaced women, how family-focused violence is exacerbated in times of war (an example is the extreme forms of incest and wife battering in the Atlantic Coast region of Nicaragua), the abuse and torture of women prisoners of war, and the behaviour of peacekeeping operations which promote sexual exploitation of women. A related question in this context is the issue of women fighters. Aside from the fundamental cultural issue of whether women should form a part of fighting forces, is it reasonable to suggest, as it has been by some people, that an army which accepts women on equal terms with men has a greater likelihood of being able to retain high standards of behaviour?

Human rights and protection issues deserve a higher profile in NGO work. They should be dealt with in a way that links international issues such as legal reform and lobbying to community level protection and support and also to looking at the active role of women in the protection of children, other women and men too. NGOs need to invest more resources in identifying existing protection mechanisms and ways of strengthening and restoring them, and in seeking out new opportunities to open up discussion of human rights issues .

iii. The emergence of new forms of organisation

As discussed previously, conflict gives rise to new social configurations in the private and public spheres. In affected communities, organisation rooted in a desire for mutual support

Fig. 3 *Key issues in understanding women's experience of conflict — a summary*

- Women's role in the survival of their families and communities is critical. Efforts to support women may be important for their own sake, but in conflict situations they are essential.

- Women's ability to survive and support others must be seen holistically, addressing issues of personal psychology, protection of and by women, economic resources and activities, community support, and national and international issues of governance, representation and human rights.

- Women's capacity to extend their economic performance depends not only on access to means of production, but also to community fora in which their needs can be addressed as equal and active community members.

- Women's health issues have to be seen in a total context of collapse of services and support systems as well as of the range and depth of suffering women experience in conflict. Women's health in conflict covers issues of psychological and social adjustment, personal integrity, injury and disability as well as physical and reproductive health.

- Conflict dramatically increases levels of violence against women, whether from the actual fighting or not. Personal violence is a major threat to women's wellbeing and hence to the integrity of communities. Violence against women must be addressed at different levels — locally, nationally and internationally, and further research should be promoted into the factors which enhance it.

- Trauma is a largely unrecognised outcome of conflict for men, women and children. It needs to be researched and measures taken to help people to recover, at both personal and community levels. Men and women may react to psychological stress differently; women may have greater needs for trusting relationships and supportive social networks, and less access to them. Meeting men's needs in overcoming trauma may be of direct benefit to women if they lead to more egalitarian relationships.

- Women's principal focus of identity tends to be the family. It is at the family level that conflict can cause women much distress and at the same time it is the family that may offer the most solace and security. Demographic imbalance — more women than men, more female-headed households — limits women's marriage prospects, and hence jeopardises individual women's status within their community.

- Women's 'invisibility', allied to the intimate nature of some of their concerns, means that identifying their needs cannot be done by superficial methods of assessment

- It is essential to recognise the positive outcomes of conflict as well as the negative ones. Women already do so through their efforts to protect, mediate and promote peace, and through their emerging organisations. New roles and new opportunities may emerge for women in times of conflict: men also have to adjust in various ways, and new arrangements and new attitudes can be judiciously nurtured by NGOs with an appropriate strategic vision.

may emerge either as a result of deliberate social strategies or because of the need individuals have for support and solidarity. In many situations women join together, either formally or informally. Informal gatherings may coalesce within refugee settlements, around medical or feeding centres, uniting women who have been through similar experiences and can understand each other. On a more formal level, women's organisations may form, often at the instigation of a few determined individuals, as in the Burma case study. These organisations may offer various forms of concrete assistance, such as health care or joint income-generating initiatives, or may lobby for specific strategic purposes. For example, women's groups in Mogadishu aim to challenge the hardening of negative attitudes towards women in an increasingly tense situation of conflict. Groups such as these may be low-profile, lacking access to communications networks favoured by international NGOs, and the latter may therefore need to search them out.

Among the various initiatives taken by women in conflict situations are efforts to promote peace and reconciliation, protection of the vulnerable, and elimination of human rights abuses. Although women's peace movements have been well documented in the North — as in the case of Northern Ireland — they exist equally in the South but have received far less attention. This aspect of women's relationship with conflict needs to be further investigated.

2.3 Changes in gender relations: power, conflict and transformation

a. The potential for social transformation

The legacy of conflict is cruel. It is very difficult for communities to reintegrate after conflict. Individuals are left with physical and emotional disabilities, communities with broken and distorted households, and nations with political sores which may take a long time to heal. Recovery from conflict is thus a critical threshold in itself; the outcome may be positive, towards rebuilding, or degenerative, towards renewed conflict. The ability of both women and men to work together in reconstruction is one of the factors which may swing the prospects of recovery in one direction or the other.

In general, experience of conflict seems to indicate that it rarely changes gender relations at a fundamental level, but simply rearranges them. This rearrangement may provide women with more practical room for manoeuvre, inasmuch as rigid conceptions of gender roles are loosened, or less room, as in the case of Afghanistani women refugees on whose movements and activities increased restrictions have been placed during exile.

In some situations, there are both losses and gains for women, if the ideology which controls them is reformulated to adjust to conflict and its aftermath. Thus the 'women in development' policy being promoted officially in Uganda has both opened up new avenues of activity for women and enhanced their economic independence, and at the same time created new ways of subordinating women's labour power to the state. Where the division of labour has actually changed to allow women more flexibility and economic freedom, this has been conceded to enable them to fulfil their responsibilities more efficiently.

In most post-conflict situations, women have failed to gain increased control over economic resources, even though their functional need for such control has increased. Currently, international initiatives such as structural adjustment programmes are leading to a reduction in support to women.

Yet changes to gender relations have undoubtedly taken place as a result of conflict. The most significant changes appear to be the loosening up of the division of labour, changes in household structure and marriage relationships, and the emergence of more and stronger women's organisations. These changes provide opportunities for more fundamental issues to be addressed through discussion and gradual acceptance of new approaches. NGOs can assist this process by helping to open up new roles for women and by using their experience of conscientisation to promote discussion.

In a minority of conflict situations, the community, instead of being overwhelmed by a set of conflicting interests over which it has little direct contact or control, is led by a movement which explicitly bases itself on people's needs. Such movements, promoting popular participation in political processes at grassroots level, may or may not adopt a strategy of positive change in the position of women. But where they do, the outcome may be dramatic. In Central America, Eritrea, and Tigray, women have gained the right to have their voices heard in political fora, to education and training in new skills, to fight in the army alongside men, and to freedom from the interference of oppressive legislation and tradition in their personal affairs.

It may be argued that these rights have not in fact succeeded in changing fundamental attitudes. Experience shows that the problems of maintaining these advances after the conflict is over are great. In Eritrea, for example, women are concerned about the assumption by male leaders that they should now return to their traditional gender role. Women with experience of political processes at the highest levels, who might be able to carve out opportunities for other women, are relatively few and have a struggle to maintain their access to funds, training, and influence. Nevertheless, strong women may serve as positive role-models who provide women with an awareness of alternative visions and allow them to develop in their own individual way.

b. Power and empowerment

This linking of analyses of conflict and gender inevitably raises questions about the simplistic image of men as perpetrators and women as victims of violence. The reality is different: while women may participate actively in wars as soldiers and support personnel, those who do not may still encourage or incite their menfolk to violence. In addition, men as well as women are often unwilling victims of war — killed and maimed, driven from their homes, and dragged off reluctantly to fight.

A more valid dichotomy between men's and women's experience of conflict lies in the fact that armed conflict involves struggles for power in which women and men are caught up in different ways, since each sex has differential, gendered access to power. Gender analysis contributes to the study of power relations by pointing out the ways in which power finds expression in the structural relations between men and women. These ways both parallel and cut across the structural imbalances of power which lead to armed conflicts. Leading from this, looking at the impact of armed conflict on women gives insights into the whole arena of conflict as the exercise of power. Traditionally, physical power and the power to control material resources have been seen as masculine attributes. Power is desirable as a means of obliging another person to do what you want them to do.

However, new perspectives on power are emerging, providing a different perspective and offering the hope that power can be seen as something which enriches us all. Empowerment and disempowerment are difficult concepts to deal with in practice. Empowerment implies entrusting people with the means — intellectual, emotional and educational as well as material — to exercise control over the decisions and resources which are important to them. Conflict is on balance more likely to disempower women than to empower them, by attacking their physical and mental health, by placing obstacles in the way of their economic self-sufficiency, and by enhancing the social attitudes which maintain their subordination. Rape, in bringing together gender, conflict and power, exemplifies the domination of the powerful over the powerless. As such, rape can be seen as symbolic of conflict.

In short, the impact of conflict on women mirrors the impact of conflict on all the more vulnerable members of a community and indeed on all vulnerable communities. The challenge of development in the context of conflict is to create the conditions where balanced interests, openly expressed and accorded respect by all, succeed in questioning imbalance and injustice and in outlawing domination, whether of women by men, or of any group over another.

Fig. 4 *Different perceptions of power*

We can distinguish between these different ways of looking at power:

Power-over: implies relationships of dominance subordination between people who have different interests, for example:

- men/women
- rich/poor
- white/black
- employer/employee
- us/them

It is based ultimately on socially sanctioned threats of violence, punitive action or intimidation, and invites both resistance and submission.

Power-to: involves developing people's skills, understanding, and problem-solving abilities. It is creative, enabling and (mostly) individual.

Power-with: is empowerment through collective organisation, common purpose and common identity. It requires the ability to act in concert and is manifested through tackling concrete problems together.

Power-within: means spiritual strength; it is the essence of humanity. It is based on self-acceptance and self-respect, which translates into acceptance of and respect for others; it recognises complementarity, strengths and weaknesses in everyone. In many cultures, it is vested in particular individuals holding spiritual power on behalf of the community.

Source: CCIC/Match *Two halves make a whole*, Ottawa, 1991

I.3 Implementing Gender-Sensitive Responses to Conflict

Section I 3 discusses implications for NGO work, looking at research and planning tools, implementation, and training

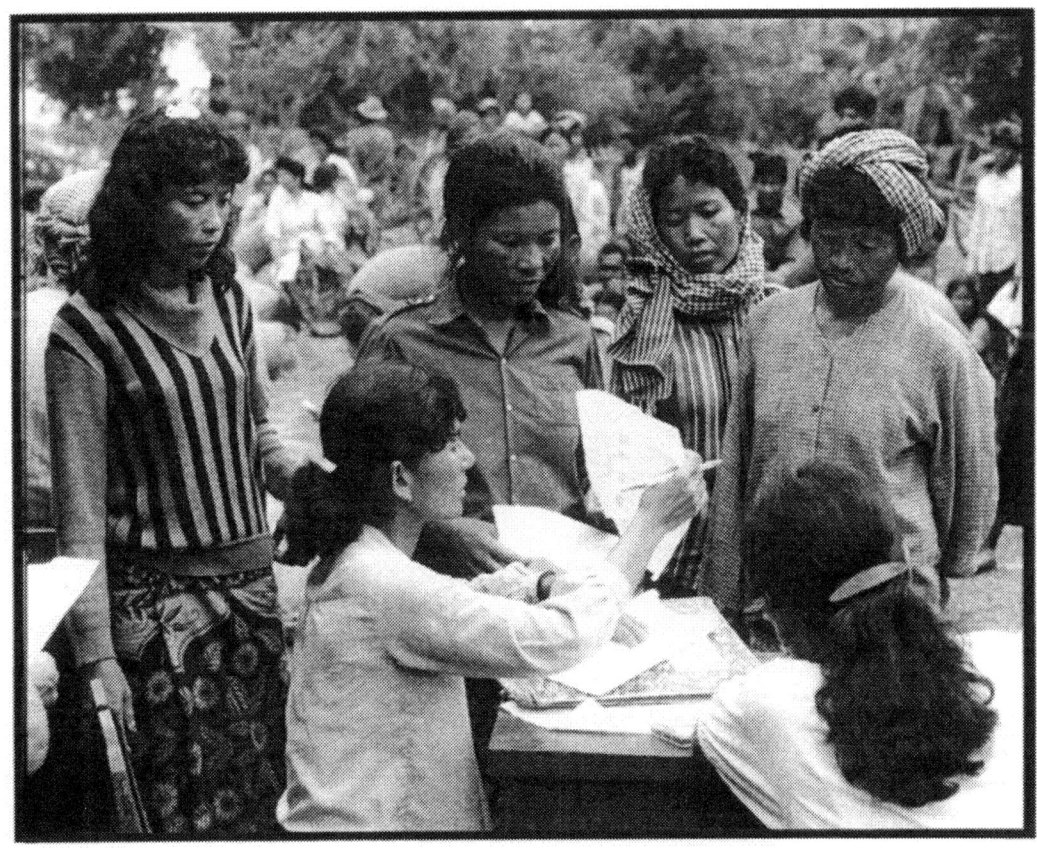

Women monitors supervising food distribution, Cambodia

3 IMPLEMENTING GENDER-SENSITIVE RESPONSES TO CONFLICT

3.1 Introduction

Working with communities overcome by war in order to support women's survival and recovery efforts is a vitally important role for NGOs working in conflict situations. Firstly, women, in the absence of men, bear responsibility for the care and protection of their families and for provision of their basic needs. Women are thus key actors in processes which will ensure the survival of future generations. Secondly, the ways in which women suffer in wars have been generally unrecognised, and are only now beginning to be understood. In particular, there is a dearth of knowledge about trauma and the impact of disability. Thirdly, the understanding of women's issues in conflict leads also to a better understanding of the mechanisms of social transformation and survival. Changes in the dynamics of gender relations triggered off by conflict may have long-lasting implications for the community's economic and social health in the future. These factors require development agencies to give clear priority to the adoption of gender-sensitive approaches in their work in conflict, both in terms of policy and in terms of practical operations.

This section examines some of the functional problem areas associated with NGO responses to conflict, looking particularly at three aspects: partnership issues and potential areas of difficulty or resistance within communities and partner agencies; institutional factors limiting flexibility and effectiveness; and issues in assessment, monitoring and evaluation.

3.2 Assessment, monitoring and evaluation

Conflict situations impose on NGOs a requirement for high quality research, meeting two needs: on the one hand, that of rapid and flexible feedback to facilitate emergency responses where appropriate, and on the other a broad, holistic view of underlying factors and long-term needs.

As the preceding sections have stressed, there is a need to approach conflict and post-conflict situations through a deeper understanding of the processes that take place within communities and how these processes interact with external factors. Yet, when dealing with emergency situations arising out of conflict, there is often also a need to prioritise immediate, practical assistance, as well as a lack of time and institutional resources to devote to research and planning. It is to be hoped that the need to reconcile these two requirements may lead agencies to adopt new policy approaches as well as amended practices in the field.

NGO practitioners working in conflict need to join up more effectively with those who are developing and refining methods of data collection and research. This is a huge and fast-moving field. New methodologies such as Participatory Rural Appraisal (PRA), popular education and auto-evaluation are establishing the importance of involving people at community level in the assessment of needs, the setting of goals, and the evaluation of progress; new analytical frameworks, including those mentioned below, are assisting practitioners to organise and direct their knowledge of situations on the ground. However, each of these methods has its own limitations, and may need to be adapted for particular

---

Fig. 5 *A gender perspective in assessing needs in conflict situations: a ten-point checklist*

1 Even if there is little time to carry out full-scale research, avoid making the assumption that everybody's needs are the same.

2 Recognise that women may be relatively 'invisible' and that conflict may keep them inside their homes more than at normal times. A determined effort may need to be made to seek out their opinions.

3 Recognise that psychological, social and cultural needs may be just as important in ensuring people's survival as the physical needs for food and shelter, and that meeting these can save lives too.

4 Seek information from a variety of different people — women as well as men, ordinary people as well as community leaders, individuals as well as organised groups, etc.

5 Use simple, flexible methods of research that don't require advanced skills or special equipment to implement; identify a small but manageable number of key indicators.

6 Identify how people are surviving through their own efforts and try to support these, rather than imposing an outsider's view of what is needed.

7 Identify the mechanisms that the community has itself put in place to assure that basic functions, including the protection of the most vulnerable, are carried out. It is normally best to work through these mechanisms, without necessarily offering them unquestioning support.

8 Identify a small number of particularly vulnerable families to monitor through regular in-depth interviews.

9 Write up your experiences and ensure that this information is shared and discussed with others addressing similar situations.

10 Adopt a disaster-preparedness strategy whereby **all** staff, including those working in areas not affected by conflict, have access to training that will strengthen their assessment, decision-making and management skills.

situations. Few have been designed from the point of view of gender-effectiveness and more work is required to develop their capacity to elicit gender perspectives. Likewise, they have not been specifically designed for application in conflict situations.

Effective and sensitive assessment of needs ideally requires a comprehensive picture of the community's situation. Frameworks for assessing needs in conflict situations should fulfil three main requirements: firstly, they should elicit an understanding of the historical development of the conflict, the factors that contributed to it at local and external levels, and the different ways in which different actors and different elements within the community have been caught up in it. Secondly, such frameworks need to address the question of resource availability, looking at the differential access to resources of different sectors of the community (men and women, leaders and others, etc) and their differential control over the use of these resources. The term 'resources' should itself be understood in its broadest sense, including political position, influence, personal qualities, social cohesion, education and skills, as well as physical and economic assets. Such frameworks may trace changes over time in the availability and use of resources, in order to understand both what has been lost through conflict and what has been retained — and also perhaps what has been gained. Lastly, needs-assessment frameworks should include an analysis of the strengths and weaknesses with which the community faces the crises that confront it. Ultimately, it is these strengths and weaknesses, rather than external assistance, which will determine the prospects for recovery.

In all these aspects, information must be disaggregated according to different groups within the community, including men and women, while recognising that divisions of class and ethnicity may cut across gender distinctions.

Monitoring and evaluation systems and methods provide agencies with criteria and indicators with which they can judge the relevance, impact and performance of their programmes. They are part of the 'feedback loop' and contribute to institutional learning and adaptation; as such, they need to be designed as an integral part of the programme approach. Within the context of a programme with a participatory, empowerment-oriented approach, monitoring and evaluation should likewise aim to empower participants by acknowledging the value of their own goals and criteria and by strengthening their ability to assess and evaluate the internal and external constraints they face. Their ability to deal with these constraints is the main factor in determining plans for NGO support to be withdrawn.

Monitoring and evaluation mechanisms must be broad-ranging enough to embrace all the different perspectives involved (including those of beneficiaries and of the agency concerned). In this sense monitoring and evaluation systems can only ever be as good as the appraisal and assessment which preceded them, since it is at these earlier stages that the different interest groups are identified.

Monitoring and evaluation for conflict situations may be used not only to generate information about the conflict itself, and processes of recovery and reconstruction, but may also be applied in pre-conflict situations, enabling project managers and their partners to predict conflicts before they happen. Project managers need to be alert to threatening crises, and aware of the existence of 'critical thresholds' at which decisions taken by the NGO may help to tip the balance towards or away from further deterioration. Evaluation and monitoring systems should help the NGO concerned — and others — to acquire foresight and preparedness in their immediate situation, and to improve learning about conflict in general.

Some analytical tools for use in assessment, monitoring and evaluation

a. Harvard analytical framework[20]

This framework, developed originally by Harvard University on the request of the US Department of State, has been adapted for a number of purposes, including an application by UNHCR for use in refugee situations. The Harvard Framework is designed to form the basis of a community gender profile. This profile is composed of three elements:

- the gender division of labour; a list of the respective tasks of men and women, including male and female children. 'Tasks' are grouped in the UNHCR version under four headings: productive activities, reproductive or household activities, social political religious activities, and protection activities.

- an 'access and control profile'; a list of the resources needed to carry out these tasks. ('Resources' includes material or economic resources, political or social resources, and time.) Then, who has access to these resources (men or women), who has control over their deployment, and who benefits from them.

- the external factors which affect the division of labour and the access and control profile of the community.

In the UNHCR version, the community profile is done twice, the first relating to the situation before the flight, the second after it. The second indicates not only what the community does and does not have, but also who has lost what and who has gained what. The comparison underlines the fact that a refugee or displaced community is unlikely to be totally destitute: it will have brought with it skills, knowledge, attitudes, values and means of organising itself, even if it has lost all its material resources. Refugees and displaced people can then be seen as active participants in the solution of their own problems.

This framework has some characteristic elements which are particularly useful. These are:

- the importance of resources in relation to responsibilities, and the distinction between access to resources and control over them. We have already discussed the importance of women being empowered to take control of the resources they need to carry out their extended family leadership functions in times of war: we now need to know in much more detail how this can happen in particular instances.

- a broad view of what the term 'resources' are: not just material ones but also less tangible things like skills and social organisation, and — most importantly for women — time.

- the idea that communities lose resources over time but also retain some and gain others. This aspect is particularly important if NGOs are to look seriously at their role in **support** rather than **providing inputs for victims**.

b. Capacities and vulnerabilities analysis[21]

This approach is an extension of some of the ideas behind the Harvard framework, and resulted from a research project carried out by some of the same people who had designed the framework. They investigated 41 different NGO projects responding to disaster situations of different kinds round the world. The underlying conclusion of the study is that though disasters may strike any community, only in certain communities will a disaster turn into a crisis, i.e. will be beyond the capacity of the community to survive it. The factors which determine the survival ability of a community are:

- its material and physical assets, such as land, climate, environment, health, skills relating to productive activities, technologies, etc;

- its social and organisational capacities, including social networks that offer support to people (family, political organisations), systems for distributing goods, services and wealth, etc. Gender issues are critical in this category since societies vary in the ways in which they include or exclude women's participation in such networks;

- its attitudinal or psycho-social strengths, for example, whether people feel victimised and dependent or buoyant and confident. This also has a strong gender connotation.

This framework recognises that different groups within the community (men and women, rich and poor etc) will present different profiles, necessitating separate analyses.

The most valuable idea reflected in this framework is the necessity for outside agencies to seek to build on the strengths of the community — both before, during and after a conflict has occurred — so as to enable it to withstand the effects of conflict with greater internal solidarity. It enables agencies engaged in emergency projects to assess how far they are addressing deep-seated and longer-term requirements.

c. The Longwe hierarchy of needs[22]

This framework is not specifically relevant to conflict situations, but may be applied to any situation as a guide to where to focus future activities. It looks at the issue of equality of access by men and women to certain key development indicators. They are:

- Control over resources
- Participation in decision-making
- Conscientisation
- Access to resources
- Well-being

These are arranged in a hierarchy with the bottom one being the focus of initial attention. The framework assumes that the objectives of women's development are ordered according to this hierarchy, i.e. equality of control of resources is not truly possible unless equality in the other four spheres has been achieved. Planners can decide where on the grid to place women's condition and position in the community concerned, and resolve to focus on the next line up, albeit bearing in mind that the ultimate goal is complete equality in all aspects.

d. Comment: comparison of methods

Each of these tools has its advantages and drawbacks, according to circumstances. The trick is to use them in combination, or to continue the work of adapting them. Briefly, the strengths and weaknesses of each are as follows:

- The Harvard Framework works best when it is looking at detail and when it is being carried out by people who have detailed knowledge of the community. In such a case it can be very informative and give fairly clear and accurate pointers to the most important short-term and long-term needs to be addressed. It brings into the analysis two factors which are of great importance to women in conflict situations and which are usually overlooked: time as a resource, and women's need for (and roles in relation to) protection. However, its weakness is that it is of little benefit if one does not have accurate, detailed information. It is also difficult to use across a region or group of communities which may not be totally homogeneous.

- Capacities and vulnerabilities analysis has the potential for generating much insight and understanding of social processes and the ways in which communities adapt to crises. The analysis can focus on sections of the community or widen its scope to regional or national level. However, it may tempt people with a relatively superficial knowledge of the situation to make guesses.

- The Longwe grid is a slightly more elaborate version of the Moser practical strategic dichotomy. But rather than a dichotomy, it presents a progression. It permits an assessment of what advantages exist in women's situation and what still has to be done. Its disadvantage is that it is static and takes no account of how situations change over time. Some of its basic assumptions (for example the one that the different stages have to be worked through in order) have been questioned.

3.3 Policy considerations in specific conflict-related situations

This section considers a number of operational contexts which present particular gender-relevant problems. The aim is to present an overview of the issues, since for the most part they are dealt with in more detail elsewhere, either in this report or others.

a. Gender and emergencies

Because emergency situations require immediate material responses, it is often difficult to ensure that the needs of all affected members of the community are adequately taken into account. Assumptions are often made about needs which are based on the previous experiences of the staff concerned and/or on research among the most visible and vociferous members of the community, rather than an assessment of a full range of needs among all sections of the community. Yet women's needs in conflict situations are not only quite various and complex, mirroring their multiple and changing social roles, but are also critically important in maintaining social cohesion and community survival during conflict and its aftermath. Ensuring that this is taken into account in practical ways requires organisational change at a number of levels: in personnel recruitment, orientation and training; in operational policy regarding the implementation of emergency activities; in research methods and feedback systems; and in the evolution of organisational policies on the role of agencies in the international community's response to conflict. Further discussion of this subject can be found in section 2.2 of this report, on women's experiences of conflict, in section 3.1 on assessment, monitoring and evaluation, and in material produced by Oxfam's Gender and Development and Emergencies units.[23]

b. Refugee and displaced women

Figures from the United Nations Commissioner for Refugees show that women and children made up around 85 per cent of the 20 million refugees in the world in 1991. If internally-displaced populations are added, the number of women and children forced to flee their homes is very much higher. Yet it is only in the last few years that the special vulnerabilities of displaced women and children have begun to be recognised.[24] Refugee situations place extreme limitations on the ability of both women and men to secure their own livelihoods, as well as having a detrimental effect on their capacity to organise mutual support. The psychological impact of refugee status is also damaging and is in turn exacerbated by other pressures. The very fact of having had to flee can itself seriously impair a person's ability to deal with these problems. In addition to the trauma of war and the loss of the home, family and community, women undergo further traumatic experiences during their flight, and further suffering as a refugee. In all three of these situations they are vulnerable to economic, political and sexual exploitation.

Clearly women and children have special protection needs, which are often not forthcoming even in communities which are under UN protection. UNHCR is under-resourced and not always convinced of the need to give priority to women's protection. However, UNHCR has been foremost in the struggle to identify policies and procedures that maximise the protection its staff can offer.[25] On the other hand, women and children who remain within the boundaries of their own countries are normally not eligible for UNHCR assistance, and indeed may be specially at risk from the very forces that have obliged them to flee in the first place.

In addition, refugee women may need a variety of special services, ranging from trauma clinics to the provision of jobs, from child care to counselling. While some women's self-image may be so deeply affected that they find it difficult to function socially at all, many (perhaps the majority) run the risk of sinking into apathy and despair unless they are encouraged to take an active role in providing for, and in decision-making about, their own futures. The case study from Sri Lanka describes a project which adapted to women's need for an active, developmental role, with positive results.

c. Demobilisation

In the 'fragile peace' which may ensue after a cease-fire, one of the major problems confronting a nation recovering from war is that of re-integrating ex-combatants (mainly men) into a society which no longer has a use for military forces. The problem manifests itself at a number of levels, for example:

- economically: viable economic activities must be identified and appropriate skills training carried out: ex-soldiers who have failed to hand in their weapons, and whose demobilisation allowances have run out, may revert to banditry or renewed involvement in conflict if they are unable to identify any other economically viable solutions.

- socially: husbands and fathers must be reintegrated into their families and encouraged to feel that they still have a role to play, even when their womenfolk have coped without them for years. Both men and women will have to adapt to changed gender roles and changed expectations of their partners.

- in public health terms: demobilised soldiers may be a source of a number of sexually-transmitted diseases, including HIV/AIDS, and may spread these through violent means. Conflict has been acknowledged as a major contributor to the spread of AIDS for this reason.

- psychologically: other public health consequences of poorly-managed demobilisation may include increases in alcoholism, domestic violence and suicide amongst men.

In cases where women have taken part in the armed struggle, such as in Eritrea, the reintegration of women fighters may also be problematic. Whereas women fighters are officially lauded and respected, and presented as an example of successful alternative role models, in practice women fighters may find it difficult to return to civilian life if this means reverting to 'feminine' stereotypes.

d. Women as peace-makers

Much has been made of the fact that wars tend to be waged mainly by men while women are said to represent peace. Such stereotypes are belied by the existence of women in the military in many countries, and by the many other types of support (logistic, cultural, economic, etc) that women give their menfolk in times of conflict. While it may be men who go to war, they may be educated and encouraged in ideals of manhood and stories of past battles and rivalries by their mothers, wives and sisters. Yet the fact remains that countless examples exist, from situations o conflict all over the world, of initiatives taken, led, or energised by women, who lend their moral force to a non-violent resolution of problems. Often these initiatives are consciously cross-cultural, linking women on both sides of a military divide, such as the Women in Black movement in Israel. The most widely-known examples of such movements are in the West, but they are known to exist in many Third World conflict zones, where international news media do not reach.

Agencies operating in conflict situations do not always have information about such movements or interest in seeking them out as partners. While some groups may be actively engaged in conflict resolution, others may prioritise mutual protection amongst women, the promotion of economic opportunities, or lobbying on issues of women's human rights.[26]

3.4 Partnership issues

Conflict tends to intensify different aspects of a community's attitudes to women: sometimes, women and others perceived as vulnerable are carefully protected, and may be sent away to places of refuge; in other cases they are left behind to fend for themselves. Their position, behaviour, and outlook may be intimately tied up with their own perceptions of personal identity and family loyalties and with culturally-defined ideals of group identity and survival. Decisions by or about women in emergency situations (where to go, how to live) are likely to be highly influenced by such intuitive factors.

The fact, for example, that Somali women's behaviour came under such intense scrutiny just at the time of the US invasion was hardly coincidental: a people whose dignity and integrity has been so sorely undermined may look to women as the last bastion of national pride and the last hope of cultural survival. Governments and agencies wishing to take a public stand on particular issues should remember to consider the potential effect of their lobbying efforts on the country's internal dynamics, including the role of women and attitudes towards them. Nor can it be assumed that such attitudes are the exclusive province of men: women may be foremost in promoting a conformist ethos.

This being the case, it needs to be emphasised that the whole issue of agency responses to women's needs may be an extremely delicate one on a cultural as well as a personal level, and needs to be handled with sensitivity and respect towards all actors.

The case studies in Part II suggest some of the problems that may arise when dealing with women's issues at community level. These include, for example, the difficulty women have in voicing their needs within community structures at times when resources are scarce, as in Somalia; the difficulty of overcoming protectionist attitudes towards women and establishing their active participation in relief and recovery activities, as in Burma; the lack of training in many community based or oriented organisations in ways of linking gender with other technical aspects of their programme, as in the Philippines; and the welfarist approaches of some partner bodies, leading to only partial recognition of the issues to be dealt with, as in Lebanon.

In the Burma case study, we see something of the difficulties of working through partners who, though concerned about women's welfare and participation, take a paternalist point of view which accords little weight to women's own perception of their problems. A similar perspective emerges from the Lebanon case study, where willingness clearly exists to promote women's welfare and foster their participation in projects, but a gender analysis is slower in coming. Here too, during the worst periods in the conflict, the needs of survival took precedence over the need to consider the long-term impact. Now, however, the existence of a peace process, however brief it may turn out to be, gives some respite for reflection and discussion on the purpose and effectiveness of interventions to be carried out. Oxfam's role of strengthening the survival capacity of local NGOs over the last decade places it in a good position to take advantage of this opportunity.

The Philippines case is somewhat different, since it describes a situation where civil society is relatively sophisticated and familiar with concepts such as gender. However, here too there is a need for Oxfam and other NGOs to play a catalysing role, enabling partners to see the connections between gender and the other aspects of their work, and to see how this work can be made more concrete and relevant in grassroots situations.

Women are, in effect, even more 'invisible' in times of war. Addressing this problem requires a twin-track approach, working on the one hand to support and strengthen emerging women's organisations and provide women with the space to develop their own understanding of their own problems, and on the other hand setting out on a long-term process of dialogue with partner organisations of all types with the goal of expanding their vision of women's position and role.

It is all too easy for partners to see the need for gender equity as secondary to other goals such as the political viability or survival of the community in the face of oppression or disaster. Important as these clearly are, the community will be constrained in meeting these goals if over half the population is living under impossible burdens. Thus the overarching goals of the society and goals of gender equity should not be seen as either-or alternatives, but as part and parcel of the same search for emancipation.

In approaching the issue of dialogue with partner organisations and communities, Oxfam and other similar agencies should give attention to the question of how they can build relationships which will enable gender to be addressed jointly in a constructive way. (The special dynamics of armed conflict pose particular difficulties for agencies which are drawn into an emergency situation only at the moment of conflict: the ethos and practice of partnership demands that NGOs establish their credibility, which can normally only be developed through a period of collaboration and the building of mutual trust over time.)

Raising gender issues with partners can either strengthen or weaken partnership. It can strengthen partnership if it is done as part of a long-term strategy of permanent dialogue: it can weaken it if based on ad hoc and peremptory decisions on the part of the funding agency. To enable partners to move forward in such circumstances, Oxfam or similar agencies need to increase their own awareness and skills in dealing with gender issues, and their ability to raise them with partners.

A long-term strategy for working with project partners should be characterised by open dialogue and a spirit of collaboration, the ability to listen to critical questions from partners, transparency, and a recognition that learning is a two-way process, the allocation of time and resources, and clear prioritisation on where to start, who to start with, why, and what are the roles and responsibilities of each. Agencies must recognise that partners face significant practical problems in discussing and dealing with these issues, and provide assistance that takes this into account.

3.5 Institutional issues

Adapting to new circumstances demands of institutions a degree of flexibility in terms of both policy and management, and the capacity to identify and deal with the internal blockages that constrain adaptability. Here we look at three aspects of internal functioning which tend to be problematic in this context: project implementation, management issues, and policy constraints. Lastly we look at some common blockages in terms of gender effectiveness.

a. Project implementation

Linda Agerbak describes how Oxfam programmes in conflict situations tend to go through four stages.[27] In the first, which she terms 'the shrinking development programme', a planned long-term programme which is gradually overcome by conflict tries in the face of increasing erosion to persevere with its current plans. In the second phase, intense violence forces a reassessment of programme aims and style. Typically, the programme moves into a 'holding operation' mode, with a much increased proportion of activities and budget going to emergency and recovery, and long-term plans being shelved. The third stage, termed 'development in conflict', is one in which the programme settles into a pattern of conflict work, redesigning activities towards social organisation and communications, and taking a more strategic look at the underlying causes of conflict. The final stage, 'planning for peace', applies to situations where the conflict has itself moved into a stage of negotiation which allows Oxfam the space to raise issues of empowerment and advocacy as well as economic recovery. The challenge of this analysis is to identify the routes by which programmes can

Fig. 6 *Possible components for a strategy for Oxfam for working with partners on gender and conflict:*

1 **Joint training workshops on gender and conflict** involving Oxfam staff and project partners, using both regionally-based resources and the resources available from within Oxfam (UK and regional).

2 **Strengthening ties with and understanding of women's organisations and movements**, since they will have information and insights about the situation of women in the country or region which will help Oxfam to develop its own country or regional perspectives and outlook.

3 Strengthening and developing a consistent **strategy for networking and information exchange** between those working on gender issues and those working on development issues in general, at country level.

4 Commissioning **research which documents and synthesises the experiences of men and women in conflict** and in **post-conflict** situations; prioritising the contracting of **local and regional researchers** for this task and **investing resources** in documentation and distribution; generally being open to funding requests from partners working on gender and conflict issues.

5 Strengthening Oxfam's **resource-base of local women consultants, trainers and experts** for employment in conflict situations, which will enhance the likelihood of culturally sensitive gender-balanced perspectives being incorporated into planning.

6 Prioritising the **integration of gender into technical issues in conflict situations**, by supporting the training of specialist gender staff to work with or in technical teams.

7 Inviting the **participation of partner groups in Oxfam meetings** and workshops.

8 Providing gender-sensitive partners with **opportunities to contribute** to the design of Oxfam's strategies in, and long-term planning for, conflict situations.

9 Encouraging Oxfam staff to develop **skills as 'trainers of trainers'**, strengthening partners' ability to explore gender issues in their own work; providing resources such as time, training and technical resources to facilitate this.

10 Exploring mechanisms whereby Oxfam can establish dialogue with partners, so that **experience on gender can be incorporated in concrete ways** during project design and implementation.

11 Encouraging the development of ties and **networking between partners on a regional or cross-regional basis**.

12 Aiming through research and practical experience to **recover the concept of gender as it is expressed in the societies in which we work**, and investigating with partners its liberating and oppressive aspects.

13 At grassroots level, **seeking out individuals holding moral and spiritual authority within the community** who share Oxfam's concern for equity and social justice, and who can become allies, and strengthening them in their work.

move from one stage into the next and the internal and external blockages that can prevent this.

Undoing the knots that tend to tie conflict programmes into rigid frameworks requires preconceptions about programme activities, style and inputs to be broadened. Agencies specialising in technical assistance or rural development, or having some other specific niche (perhaps long argued over and hard-won), may find it difficult to embrace new roles that are far removed from their old ones, such as conflict resolution, mediation, or rape counselling. But this may be the sort of challenge that conflict imposes. Agencies in this position may be facing difficult choices: it may not be helpful to a community engulfed in conflict to be assisted by external agencies that have neither been through their traumatic experiences, nor can offer the skills and competencies which are needed in the new circumstances. Thus the prevalence of conflict in the Third World creates critical thresholds for development agencies as well as for the communities concerned.

Organisations wishing to continue working in conflict must fulfil certain requirements in terms of flexibility, openness and skill development, which are related to management systems.

b. Management issues

Organisations with highly centralised management structures and project approval, and funding mechanisms may find it difficult to develop flexible responses to conflict. Local teams are often expected or obliged to respond to rapidly changing circumstances on behalf of the agency without having an opportunity to discuss, plan, or seek approval. Indeed, they may be out of contact with their line management for days or weeks at a time. Staff on the ground must therefore be trained, confident, and entrusted with the responsibility to make decisions and take initiatives. The parameters within which they can operate should be clearly defined beforehand as part of a 'disaster-preparedness' strategy.

The 'front-line', consisting of locally-based staff and partners, is even more of a resource to the agency during conflict than at other times, and repays a considerable investment in terms of support and training. Others involved in the management of conflict programmes, further up the line-management system, also have support needs which should not be overlooked. Staff overload is a frequent problem: the issues of workload and stress management for staff engaged in conflict projects are important.

'Front-line' staff in conflict situations generally need to be able to communicate directly with communities. They should be of the right sex, and language group, and have the level of inter-personal skills to facilitate this communication with all sections of the community — not just those who are more accustomed to talking to outsiders. Gender awareness should be a main criterion for staff recruitment. This recommendation is essential if a holistic view of community needs and capacities is to be obtained, and is especially important for improving gender-sensitive responses.

Inflexible programme planning, and maintaining a rigid distinction between 'emergency' and 'development' activities are not conducive to flexible responses. Staff need to be in touch with what other sections of the organisation are doing and thinking, and encouraged to share experiences. Monitoring frameworks need to be adapted to conflict situations, and monitoring visits need to made more frequently than usual.

c. Policy responses

At policy level, a breadth of vision about possible responses to conflict is required, and one which looks realistically to the future to foresee possible needs in terms of budgets, training needs, and policy frameworks. In short, a 'disaster-preparedness' strategy is required. The need to re-examine rigid categories and assumptions, such as those separating 'emergency' from 'development' activities, is paramount.

Policy discussions must be oriented towards examining the trends, patterns and root causes behind different types of conflict. NGOs must seek to identify what strategies each one of them can adopt to help communities to unpick the threads of violence that tie them into cycles of conflict. Concepts such as empowerment, governance, and the nature of civil society need to be explored, and ways of furthering them in specific situations placed on the agenda of assessment and research activities.

Lastly, policy responses to conflict need to be seen not only in relation to project activities on the ground but as part and parcel of all the facets of an NGO's operations, including public policy and lobbying work, development education, and fundraising activities. Linkages between the concerns of the grassroots of the Third World and those of Northern publics and governments are not hard to find; they need forming and identifying in terms of human rights, international trade and debt, structural adjustment policy, EC agricultural policy, the arms trade, and countless other issues. Information and experience from NGO programmes should be the basis for public policy initiatives, which in turn must faithfully reflect the realities of people's lives.

d. Particular blockages on gender

The logic of the preceding sections is that NGOs must expand their capacity in gender work if they are to respond adequately to the needs of conflict situations. Critical pathways in this expansion relate to policy development, training, and management and staffing issues. At the policy level, it needs to be recognised that all aspects of an organisation's work contain gender implications. This includes supposedly technical areas, such as water supply or budgeting. There is no such thing as a gender-neutral issue. Policy development must take into account the specific gender aspects of each sector. This has major implications for emergency planning, a sector which is often regarded as being determined by the urgency of the response required and the need for efficiency in delivery. Training in gender awareness in conflict situations needs to reflect not only the basic concepts of gender and development approaches but also specific adaptations for different types of work, in order to ensure that the organisational ethos is infused into them. In particular, expatriate staff need to be made aware not only of general concepts and policies in terms of gender, but also of how these are interpreted within specific cultural and political settings. Women staff and gender specialists need to be in place in field programmes and at key positions in management and monitoring functions. They need to have clearly defined roles within the management structure, and to be able to influence decisions about planning and resource allocation. Staff in a position to use or manage significant resources should have their job descriptions reviewed to ensure that a gender perspective is incorporated.

Fig. 7 *Institutional factors in enhancing gender sensitivity in conflict responses*

In summary, a development agency can best enhance the suitability of its response if it:

- has the capacity to reflect on, reconsider, and broaden the basic building blocks of policy and has the internal communications structures which maximise this learning capacity;

- has the capacity and the will to incorporate gender into strategic planning and policy design;

- has the capacity to listen to, value and support what men and women in conflict areas are saying and doing about their own situation and needs, and involve them actively in projects;

- avoids the 'emergency mentality' in which assumptions about the role of NGOs as essential to survival go unquestioned;

- promotes decentralised decision-making i.e. empowers well-trained and confident groups of front-line staff to make rapid responses to local emergencies;

- invests in training, sharing and exchange of experience and knowledge with and between partners (and staff);

- ensures that women staff are employed at key front-line, managerial, and policy-making positions, and are adequately trained and supported;

- develops clear frameworks for monitoring and evaluating its impact and sets clear goals and indicators accessible to staff and partners.

II. A The Impact of Armed Conflict on Gender Relations

    1. Cambodia
    2. Somalia
    3. Uganda

Civil war in Somalia

Vince Coultan/Oxfam

II CASE STUDIES

A: THE IMPACT OF ARMED CONFLICT ON GENDER RELATIONS

Case Study 1: CAMBODIA

Pok Panhavichetr

Background

For the last 20 years Cambodia has been involved in conflict:

1970-1975: bombing of part of Cambodia by Americans because of Vietnam war
1975-1979: Dictatorship by Khmer Rouge led by Pol Pot
1979-1991: Civil war between four factions
1991 onwards: Preparations for election in May 1993.

The social status of women

1 The status and role of women in Cambodian society

As a result of the civil war and hostilities in Cambodia over 20 years, the economic situation of Cambodian women continues to worsen. Women bear exceptionally heavy responsibilities in the socio-economic life of Cambodia. The tragic events of 1970-1979 and the on-going hostilities have left Cambodia with a population in which adult women (above 18 years of age) account for 60-65 per cent of the population.

Since the onset of socialist rule in 1979, official policy in Cambodia has been that men and women are equal. However, in reality women are not valued equally. For instance, women who graduated as engineers often work in the office as book-keepers, typists or tea-makers rather than as extension workers in the factory. In the community, women are not involved in decision-making, men are always stronger and more respected.

Traditionally, Khmer women have always borne heavy responsibilities in society from a very early age. At birth, a girl was sometimes looked upon as a burden to the family and a cause for worry. A daughter can do many more things to embarrass the family than a son. Girls are even compared to pieces of cotton wool, while boys are likened to diamonds, since a diamond can be dropped into mud, picked up and washed clean; however, cotton wool can never return to its original purity once dropped into mud, no matter how much cleaning is done.

A girl rarely completes primary education, instead helping to care for younger brothers or sisters or helping with household, agricultural and other productive works, until her parents chose a husband for her.

2 Women's economic strategies

When she gets married, a Cambodian woman takes on the important role of wife and mother. As a wife, she handles the family budget and is responsible for borrowing money if the family needs it; she is also responsible for all the housework. While her husband is seen as the breadwinner and usually supervises children's formal education at school, the wife is entirely responsible for their overall upbringing and health and will be held responsible for failure. Most women have to earn money to support the family, in addition to, or instead of, a male wage.

Between 30 and 35 per cent of households are headed by women. Of these, some are widows whose husbands died in the war during the Lon Nol or Pol Pot period, whereas some live with handicapped husbands, some are divorced, and others are single. As in any other country, families headed by women alone experience difficult economic conditions, a situation which is aggravated here because of Cambodia's particularly low socio-economic level. Some women heads of households have to bring up five or six children on their own.

The problem of how to support the family is particularly acute for urban women. Invariably a husband's earnings alone cannot cover the whole of the family's needs. Even government employees have a very low income. Thus all women try their best to earn money even after marriage. Some women who are government employees try to work extra time as a teacher at private schools or engage in another income-generating activity.

The informal sector, i.e. street vendors and market sellers, is almost completely run by women. Women who have capital can run bigger businesses selling gold or running other types of shops. Most women can only run small-scale businesses, such as selling prepared food, sweets, fruit, vegetables, fish or groceries from market stalls or on the pavement. Because of lack of skills or capital for running business, some women hire themselves to wrap candies in private shops, a task for which they are paid only small amounts of money. Some others, especially women heads of households (widows, divorced) have to work in what are considered in Cambodia to be men's jobs, such as construction works or carrying rice sacks or salt sacks at the port. Such unstable work does not allow women to save money, or to mobilise additional resources in order to move on into other business. They are living from hand to mouth, despite the amount of work they put in every day.

In rural areas the majority of women take part in agricultural production, particularly rice-growing. Women traditionally do most of the sowing, transplanting, harvesting, threshing and storing. Ploughing and harrowing were once tasks which were done by men, but now it is not very unusual to see women behind a plough because some families have no men to do this type of work. In particular, most women-headed households have no draft animals and are obliged to hire a ploughing team, which will first plough its own land before being available for hire, as a result of which women can start rice cultivation only late and therefore produce less. If women have no money to pay for ploughing they engage in 'exchange labour', asking a neighbour to plough their land in return for help with transplanting. One morning of ploughing is repaid by two or three days of transplanting. Alternatively, they have to pay him in cash or rice, which is difficult for the poor. Some poor women hire themselves as agricultural labourers for transplanting and harvesting to get payment in cash or rice.

3 Problems affecting displaced women

Over 100,000 persons are displaced in Cambodia. Displaced women have specific problems. In particular, women-headed households have problems when they have to flee their villages because of shelling or fighting. They have no men to help with carrying children and household goods, and they often have to leave most of their belongings behind. After fleeing they face the problems of having no earnings; sometimes this forces them to go back to their homes, no matter how insecure or unsafe these are, to try to harvest crops and even to stay overnight there, leaving their children behind.

Women who have to flee from their village just after having delivered a baby, often find that their breastmilk production stops, so that they cannot feed their baby.

4 The status of women without male partners

Conflict has led to an imbalance in the ratio of women to men in Cambodia, which is causing a decrease in the value of women. Single, divorced, or separated women and widows do not only lose out economically but are looked down upon and are sometimes open to ridicule in Cambodian society. In the last decade, many single or widowed women have not been able to find a husband because of the shortage of men. They have been faced with the dilemma of either becoming the second or third wife of a man or of remaining alone. This is why some women choose to become second or third 'wives' — a position which is not recognised legally — sharing the father of their children with other women. This obviously makes them emotionally and economically insecure.

After the Pol Pot period, problems with unsatisfying and unhappy marriages showed up among those couples who had been forced to marry by the Khmer Rouge government. Most of these couples have been treated very badly by their parents-in-law, who forced their children to separate in order to marry someone of the family's own choosing. Again, deserted wives are disadvantaged and must choose to remain precariously single or 'remarry' into a polygamous relationship.

Traditionally Cambodians take a very strict view of relationships between men and women. It is acceptable for men to have girlfriends, whereas the mere idea of unfaithfulness is unthinkable for women. For example, if a woman who is a government employee 'misbehaves', she may be demoted or deprived of her job, whereas a man will simply receive a warning.

If husbands become handicapped, wives normally continue to live with their husbands as an ordinary family, but handicapped women can often not keep their husbands. They are often left with their children while their husbands marry a new woman, and have to live without support from their husbands, making their lives even more difficult.

5 Prostitution

Casual relations with women and prostitutes outside married life is a usual aspect of urban culture. Until recently, many of the prostitutes in Phnom Penh were Vietnamese women who migrated from Ho Chi Minh city to escape poverty. However, currently there seems to be an increasing number of young Khmer women coming from the provinces to engage in prostitution in the capital. Reasons for prostitution include the need to repay debts, or to support families back in the provinces. While widows or abandoned women have young children to support, war orphans may have to support younger brothers and sisters. The problem of prostitution has become bigger since UNTAC arrived in Cambodia.

6 Solidarity among women

Because of the many years of fighting and the fundamental disruption of communities and families during the Khmer Rouge period, solidarity among Cambodian men and women is very limited. In critical situations, even today, people mainly care for their individual safety and wealth. The forced social organisation during the years of socialism have not helped to improve this situation. As a result, solidarity and mutual trust, which form the basis for mutual assistance among people everywhere, are very weak. This discourages the spontaneous formation of local initiatives and groups for joint-improvement of status and living conditions.

Conclusion

Women's position in Cambodia is subordinate to that of men. The war has increased the problems for many women, either by decreasing their value even further as they outnumber men, or by creating serious difficulties in earning a living. Single women, including widows and the handicapped, are pushed to the margins of Cambodian society. Lack of mutual trust and support inhibits the growth of local initiatives and groups to promote gender equity and attack the roots of women's inequality.

Case Study 2: SOMALIA

Judy El-Bushra

Background

The Somali nation is spread through five countries of the Horn of Africa, divided by boundaries imposed by colonial divisions. Somalis are predominantly pastoral people, living in a desert environment which is very prone to drought, though towards the south of Somalia greener vegetation permits a variety of different livelihoods including agro-pastoralism and settled agriculture.

The clan system forms the basis of society and its breakdown has been one of the main factors in the current civil war. A clan is a group of people descended from a common ancestor and claiming priority access to a certain piece of land and its resources (such as water and grazing). Clans are divided into sub-clans and even smaller divisions. Although each clan has its own territory, in practice before the war people were scattered throughout the country, often living in peace as minorities within the territory of another clan. The clan system was held together by a number of factors that created checks and balances, preventing any one clan or individual from acquiring inordinate power. These factors included neighbourhood, the sharing of natural resources, intermarriage, and trade links.

The breakdown of the clan system came about as a result of colonial interference and through 20 years of manipulation by the previous government, headed by ex-president Siad Barre. The current civil war began in 1988 in the north of the country and worked its way south, breaking out in the capital, Mogadishu, at the beginning of 1991. The north-west (the ex-British colony) later declared itself the independent state of Somaliland.

One of the main effects of the war was to cause the movement of people back to their clan territories, the only places where they could feel safe. In some cases, people had to move several times, as the fortunes of the different armed forces changed. Another change was that government collapsed, and with it all service and supply systems. Even for those people who were not obliged to move, production (agricultural and livestock) soon broke down through lack of supplies and through insecurity: animals and crops were looted, and people lost the confidence they needed to carry on producing. All this led eventually to widespread famine, which earned Somalia world-wide publicity, and which still continues, although on a reduced scale.

However, some systems have survived. The clan elders, a traditional male authority structure which had been almost suppressed during Siad Barre's regime, took over the responsibilities of local government in many areas. Petty trade, mostly carried out by women, continued as long as there was anything to be sold. Big businessmen also continue to flourish, now controlling the profitable trade in arms, food, and drugs.

Changes in gender relations

1 Trapped in their own homes

Traditionally conflict between clans was regulated by certain 'rules of engagement' which ensured that friction was kept within limits and the vulnerable did not suffer. Fighting was carried out only by men; a code of honour ensured the women and children of any clan were protected. During the present conflict there have been many examples of this code being followed, but equally there have been examples where women and children living as minorities within the territory of an opposing clan have been massacred, and it seems that this code has at least in part been abandoned.

Loss of mobility is a major constraint on women's ability to fulfil their family responsibilities in the present circumstances. Fear of rape or shooting prevents women from leaving their homes, and attacks on women are now so common that many women have taken to wearing all-enveloping Islamic dress as some degree of protection. People who stand in food queues (mostly women and older men) run a strong risk of being caught in the cross-fire if gunmen attack the food as it arrives; local women encouraged relief agencies to provide cooked food wherever possible. During the worst periods of the war, lack of clothes was another reason why women confined themselves to their houses. Women who need to work on their farms or sell goods in the marketplace prefer to go out only at midday when the danger is less. Lack of services and supplies means that women have further than usual to go for water. In one town, a dozen women have been killed by crocodiles while fetching water from the river, since there was no fuel to operate water pumps.

2 Impoverished by aid

In to the absence of men, women have taken on responsibilities for maintaining and providing for the family. This is nothing new for Somali women, many of whose menfolk have worked away from home (in the Gulf states, for example) for decades. But in the present circumstances, when food, money and other basic necessities have been difficult to come by, providing for a family has been exceptionally difficult. Almost the only avenue open to women is petty commerce, and this has been limited by the lack of produce to sell and by the lack of money circulating in the economy.

In addition, food aid has brought its own problems. In some places farmers who have a marketable surplus have been unable to get a price for their produce which covers the production costs, since food aid has depressed prices. Food aid has put many women retailers out of business, especially in the major cities where food distributions are relatively regular. At the same time, people just a few kilometres away are dying of starvation because they are not on the main routes for relief convoys.

The conflict between different clans has had a very divisive effect on the whole Somali community, breaking up friendships and families even among those who have sought refuge outside Somalia. Owing to the general preference for marrying outside the clan, there are many families in which husband and wife are from opposing clans. Many such marriages have been unable to withstand the pressures this has created. When marriages break up in this way, women are affected differently from men since they run the risk of being separated or alienated from their children, who belong to the clan of their father, as well as from their husband.

3 More work, no voice

Despite the increased responsibility women have had to shoulder as family providers, they have not always found it easy to gain access to the resources they need to meet this responsibility. Councils of elders consist exclusively of men, and there is no place for women in the taking of major community decisions. Men have tended to resist suggestions that women should join committees or take part in decision-making about resources.

Though the elders have generally taken seriously their responsibility to protect and defend the interests of those in their care, there are nevertheless many women who for one reason or another cannot claim the protection of well-placed elders. Some observers have remarked that women heads of households report the number of their dependents honestly, while men tend to inflate the numbers to receive more than their fair share of rations; and, in general, women have difficulty in pushing for their own and their family's interests.

The existence of elders' councils and other male-dominated committees in many localities poses a dilemma for agencies trying to assist the Somali community to recover from the present crisis: on the one hand, the elders have proved to be instrumental in ensuring the survival of many communities and must be supported if genuine recovery is to take place; on the other, an appropriate way must be found for the elders to take greater account of women's vital contribution and need for access to mainstream resources.

Women's behaviour has been under stricter control since the coming of foreign troops to Somalia to oversee relief distribution. One woman who was suspected of being over-friendly with French soldiers was stripped, beaten and imprisoned, to be rescued eventually by a women's organisation. A representative of the organisation was reported as saying that the incident 'highlights the powerlessness and lack of respect for women in this society'.

4 Positive changes brought about by war

Despite the problems women have faced, the war has brought some positive changes too. The dependence of many families on women's capacity to earn income and manage family affairs has brought about a widespread acceptance of new roles for women. Many women have been able to develop more balanced relationships with their husbands and often declare they do not want to go back to how things were before.

5 When the state resumes power, how will it respond to women?

In the absence of a national government one cannot talk of the state in Somalia. In future, however, the apparatus of the state will reappear. It is difficult to predict whether the war will have had a lasting effect on social attitudes towards women. Pessimists point out that the previous government had generally positive policies towards women's rights and had introduced legal changes (in women's status in marriage and divorce, for example) which were generally advantageous towards women; many of these policies may in future be discredited by association. However, the present situation contains some positive signs, such as the emergence of genuine women's organisations for mutual support.

Conclusions

The situation of women in Somalia highlights the vital needs that women have in conflict situations: particularly for personal protection and for safe access to the means to continue economic activity, whether it be agriculture, animal rearing or commerce.

Male attitudes towards women appear to be still in a state of flux. On the one hand, conservative views of women's roles and behaviour have been strengthened. On the other hand, circumstances have in many cases obliged men to acknowledge with greater respect the burdens taken on by women and the contributions they have made to the survival of family and community.

Opportunities exist in even the most desperate situations. Community mechanisms can be very resilient and building on them offers the best hope of guaranteeing people's survival both in the short and long term.

Case Study 3: UGANDA

Judy El-Bushra

Background

Uganda suffered a series of brutal and destructive civil wars and despotic regimes from the late 1960s till the mid-1980s. It is well endowed with agricultural resources, though these were all but destroyed during the war years, when people fled from their lands, and huge numbers of animals were killed.

The present government subdued most of the country in the mid-1980s and since then has installed a system of popular representation, and overseen a substantial return to production. Insurgency and insecurity continued to exist until recently in the north, but now appear to have ended. The country's struggle to regain economic viability puts enormous strain on the small rural producers who form the majority of the population, caught between their own subsistence needs and the needs of the country to collect taxes and to produce for export.

Changes in gender relations

1 Pre-conflict gender relations

Until about 20 years ago, gender relations among many Ugandan population groups were characterised by a clear division between men's and women's tasks and between the resources each needed to perform them. In northern Uganda, for example, men took responsibility for livestock, over which they had total control, and for the cultivation of cash crops which were used to underwrite the family's expenses such as taxes, school fees, clothes, and basic household supplies. Women helped their husbands on the family farms, following a fairly strict division of labour in which the heaviest tasks were reserved for men. Women also kept fields of their own, from which they supplied the family's subsistence needs; they alone worked on these fields and controlled the consumption of the produce, which was never sold and which men had no access to.

This division was backed up by a framework of marriage dominated by the husband's authority but within which wives had certain defined rights, upheld by the clan and the community. From the legal point of view, marriage was indissoluble, except by the repayment by the wife's family of the bride-wealth that had been paid by the husband. Until this happened, the husband and his clan had total control over the wife's productive and reproductive capacity i.e. neither her produce, her belongings, nor her children were her own, and the burden of supporting her and her children economically fell on her husband and his family. Many Ugandan communities practised the inheritance of widows by the surviving brother of a deceased husband; a widow who refused this arrangement would not only have to fend for herself but would be entirely dispossessed by her husband's family, and stripped of all except — and sometimes including — the clothes she stood up in.

2 Changes in the past two decades

Since then, various factors have had an impact on gender relations to create an arrangement in which women have the greater share of responsibility and work, yet still the same limited control over resources, and few enabling rights. These factors include the war and male labour migration (leading to women being obliged to take over many previously male functions), and the increasing pressures to find cash which have resulted in even women's food crops being sold. Loss of oxen through war also adds to the family's agricultural labour burden.

3 Changes since the cessation of war

The personal status of women has in certain respects changed for the better. The ending of the war and the disbanding of armed camps has lowered the risks of violence and rape from soldiers; economic opportunities for women have opened up and there is a generally increased recognition of the importance of their role. However, there are numerous exceptions to this, and levels of domestic and other forms of violence against women are still high. Abused women have few refuges: the common understanding among both women and men is that violence is part of marriage and women have no choice but to tolerate it. Likewise, women who have been raped, especially if they become pregnant, may not be able to count on the sympathy of their families.

4 An increased imbalance between men and women

Within the family, the division of labour has changed from being a relatively clear one to being blurred. Women may have to clear land or perform other traditionally male agricultural tasks in men's absence, while men have moved into women's activities wherever there is a profit to be made by doing so. Women have also tended to lose access to their own subsistence land because of the need to concentrate family labour on cash crops, a factor which has sometimes had alarming consequences for food security and for the environment.

Whereas previously it was regarded as a husband's responsibility to pay children's school fees and provide basic household necessities, these are now regarded as women's responsibilities. The need to find cash for family expenses imposes an additional labour burden on women, who habitually work without rest from dawn to night while their husbands are free for the latter part of the day to engage in leisure pursuits. Women often provide their husbands with spending money, which they may use to buy beer, (often coming home drunk and beating their wives) or save so as to marry additional wives. This labour burden is a serious constraint to women's full participation in the lives of their families as well as their communities. However, there are increasing numbers of men who recognise this problem, many of whom seek to share the burden of domestic work with their wives in spite of being ridiculed for doing so.

5 Violence and unhappiness in the private sphere

The imbalance between women's and men's work is one of several factors which have led to increased fragility of marriage, and unhappiness in marriage figures very highly in women's accounts of their problems. Fear of violence and of rejection by husbands is a major cultural undercurrent visible in the songs and poems sung by women. Women married to violent or indolent husbands may decide to continue in unhappy marriages because they seek the respectability that married status brings or because they are offered no sympathy or help from their own families.

The dispossession of widows (of whom there are now many) continues, but the custom is now widely seen as a contributory factor to the spread of AIDS and is tending to be practised less often. This in itself is problematic for some widows, who may have no means of support other than from their husband's family.

6 Changes within communities

In the past, responsible behaviour on the part of men, women and young people was sanctioned by the community. Community pressures have all but disappeared and this has had both welcome and unwelcome effects. On the one hand, brutal punishments such as those meted out in cases of unmarried pregnancy (to the girl and to the boy if he could be identified) are no longer practised. On the other hand the moral education of children is increasingly neglected, while violent or unreasonable husbands may no longer be held up to criticism as in the past.

In some areas of the country, especially in the north where camps of armed soldiers of various armies have been in existence, there is a growing problem of 'camp followers' —

women who have no means of support other than to attach themselves to garrisons, providing sexual favours for the armed forces. Many of these women have been rejected by their communities after being raped — perhaps by the soldiers themselves — or have been repudiated by their husbands, and have been unable to rely on the support of their families.

A positive outcome of the present development outlook of the country is the widespread acceptance of women's role in community affairs. Women are influential in local government and there are a large number of women's groups of different sorts which play important community roles. Women are widely represented in community-based groups, both women's groups and mixed groups.

7 Conflict and AIDS

No consideration of gender relations in Uganda can be complete without mentioning AIDS, which is now affecting every village and every section of the community. As is well-known now, women are affected by AIDS not only through their own sexual relations but also as mothers and grandmothers of AIDS patients. There is little doubt that the disruption of the war and the post-war years, and the continued presence of camps of armed forces in some parts of the country, have contributed substantially to the spread of the disease.

8 The role of the state

The present Ugandan government has put much weight behind its policy of encouraging the participation of women in all areas of national life. A women's ministry has been set up to review projects and ensure that women's needs are taken care of. A minimum number of women is required in local government councils at all levels in addition to the inclusion of specific women's representatives. A constitutional commission is reviewing, amongst other things, women's legal rights, which should be enshrined in the new constitution.

The implementation of such positive policies is beset by many constraints, not least the lack of funds, from which all government initiatives suffer, and the even greater lack of resources allocated specifically to women's activities. Moreover, the Women in Development policy as interpreted by the government has been criticised for being focused on encouraging women into ever more intensive income-generation, thus increasing their burden of work, without making concomitant changes in their position in society or in their control of resources.

Conclusions

The division of labour in Uganda has become much more flexible following the war. As in Cambodia, this has come about through necessity and has resulted in a huge burden of work for women.

Ugandan women, whether in marriage or single heads of families, have had to take responsibility for managing and providing for their families. The ending of the war has not resulted in this burden being lifted.

Violence against women is still common, and is a function of the levels of violence in society as a whole and of the lack of respect for women in general.

Government policies and pronouncements have had a very positive effect in enabling women to take wider public and family roles. However, since they have been focused on increasing women's productivity, they have not tended to amount to much more than an increasing imposition of work on women.

II. B The Effects of Conflict on Women

    4. An overview
    5. A checklist

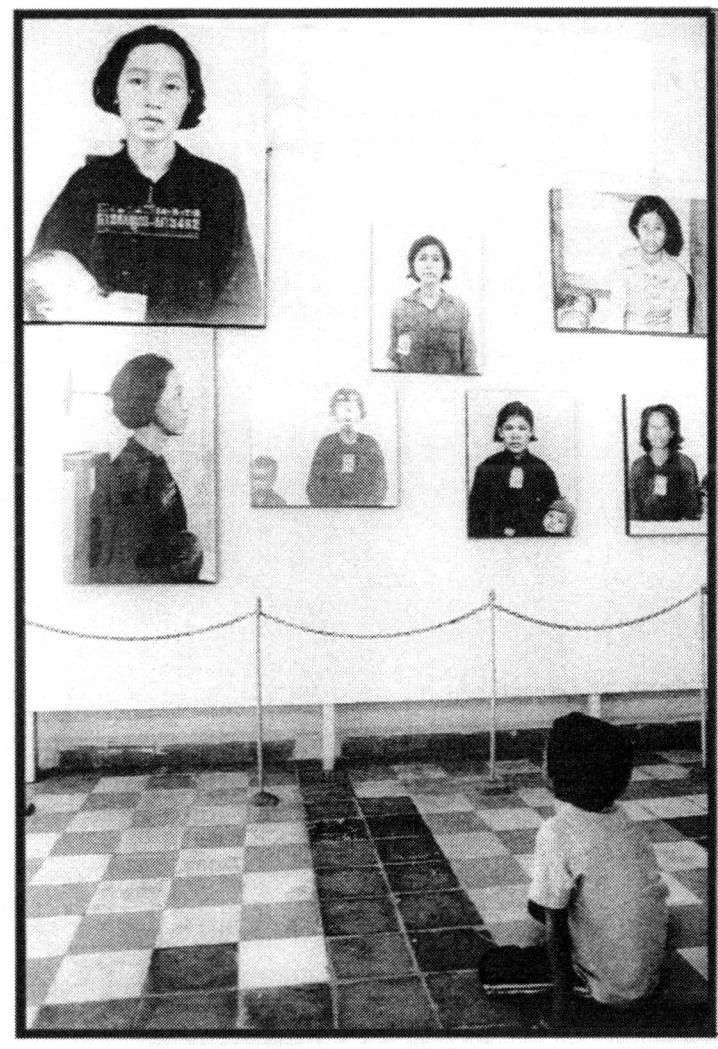

Before torture and killing Khmer Rouge took photos of their victims

B: THE EFFECTS OF CONFLICT ON WOMEN

Case Study 4: AN OVERVIEW

Claudia Garcia-Moreno

Introduction

Women have many roles apart from that of mother and family organiser, and single women are particularly at risk of both direct and indirect effects of conflict. However, most of the research that exists has been done on refugee women and focuses on their family role. This paper will have two main sections: one on general issues which will summarise some of the main concerns around the needs of women refugees, as many of them also apply to conflict situations. The second section covers some research done on psychosocial issues amongst women refugees. The paper used some examples from Cathy Mears' experiences and a few of my own.

Women's roles

1 Mothers and family organisers

Women can be direct victims of violence, and in particular suffer sexual abuse and rape. (Rape has increasingly become a common tactic in conflict.) In addition, women can be targeted through the victimisation of their children or other family members so that although they may remain physically unharmed they still suffer the consequences.

2 Providers

The economic responsibilities for the family also often fall on women, particularly after they have escaped the conflict. The stress of day-to-day survival is added to the stress of the conflict they have run away from. In situations of exile or refugee camps, women and men have to adopt new roles, at times leading to conflict in the family. For example, in the case of Afghan women in Pakistan, exile may mean more restrictions on women's movements and less economic activity outside the home; in others it may mean women become the breadwinners.[28]

3 Community organisers

Lastly, women can have an important role in resolving conflicts. They often have not been involved in decisions that lead to the conflict, but they may have a role in nurturing values of reconciliation among their children.

Particular problems facing women

All those affected by conflict suffer the problems of direct physical violence to themselves or family members, as well as those related to displacement. If refugees they suffer also the difficulties of adapting to a new environment, often a new language and culture. Women face particular difficulties because of their role as providers for the children and the family, for example, learning to cook with new ingredients.

Most of the wars going on today affect civilian populations. Torture, bombing, massacres and rape are being reported from Somalia, Bosnia, Liberia to Uganda. Women may be targeted for their own political activities, but often it is a way of getting at their men or because they are women. Pregnant women have been specifically targeted in Liberia and Uganda, for example. Women may also be harassed because they don't confirm to the cultural norms of behaviour and in particular they may face rape and abuse not only at the hands of those they flee from, but also from those from whom they seek protection. At borders or in camps where food distribution may be in the hands of army commanders or others they may be forced to have sex in exchange for passes or food rations.

Elizabeth Ferris points out that although protection is the mandate of UNHCR and there is international recognition of violence against refugee women, there is very little documentation.[29] Many of the cases are not followed up systematically and many are not even reported.

1 Practical considerations for women refugees

All refugees have the same needs for health, education and social services, and sources of economic support. However, for women to be able to use these services, the provision of childcare, the opening and closing times of clinics, and relevance of the service to their needs will be critical. For example, women may be put off from using the health services because there are only male health workers. Or they may simply be too busy to be able to participate.

Sanitation services, like latrines may be particularly important as women may not be able to defecate in open fields. For example, in Bangladesh it is reported that, until latrines were built, the Rohingya women refugees were only able to defecate after dark. In Sudan, women had to go in groups because they went at dusk, had to go a long way, and were afraid of being harassed or raped. The same may be true for bathing/washing areas.

Clothing may be particularly important as women may be too embarrassed to come out of their huts if they have no clothes. This has been reported in Mozambique, Uganda and more recently in Somalia. Cathy Mears reports that the Mundari women in Juba were happy to wear their goatskins in their homelands, but when they were displaced to the town they felt they needed clothes. The NGO workers faced the dilemma of whether to provide them with Arabic clothes (i.e. from the 'enemy culture') or to support them in the preservation of their own cultural identity.

In Liberia Oxfam was involved with UNICEF in supplementary feeding programmes for malnourished children and adults. When the malnutrition rate was very low there was great resistance to closing the programmes down because they had been more than feeding centres; they had served as *refuges* for women coming into town desperate, traumatised, and weak. Women could sit with their children in relative security. They, in effect, had permission to sit and absorb the experience. Usually, the woman in charge had also experienced some level of trauma. Cathy Mears reports that the supervisor would often talk about the past and probable future horrors — what will become of these children? How could this have all happened? There may be a case for having multi-purpose 'centres' — refuges for women to talk, rest, come together in safety. In times of conflict these can be justified through health work (explicitly or implicitly).

Health work can be a good entry point to working in a situation of conflict, and sometimes the presence of external workers can provide local people with some cover. However, it is not without its difficulties. Cathy Mears describes two situations in Luwero, Uganda where NGO workers were able to protect in one case and inadvertently endanger a woman in another. In one case a woman begged the NGO workers to take her sixteen-year-old daughter to the capital because she had been raped several times by soldiers. Full of trepidation, they hid her in the vehicle under blanket and told soldiers at the road blocks she was bleeding and about to miscarry. Because of this they were allowed through, presumably not because of compassion but because of repulsion at the thought of the miscarriage.

The second example refers to a woman and her malnourished child who needed to get to a feeding centre. The NGO took them both to the village where the centre was and had to introduce the woman to the military commander. At that point they realised they had inadvertently exposed that woman to high risk but it was too late to get her out. It was almost impossible to follow up what happened. In retrospect it seemed that the woman had agreed to move but may have thought the NGO could offer more protection than it had power to do.

2 The need for involvement

The need for women and men to feel that they have some control of their situation highlights the need for them to be involved in the planning and implementation of interventions. In this planning process it is important to ensure that women's specific needs are identified and addressed. UNHCR has produced guidelines and checklists to guide field staff on this.[30]

Often it may be difficult to get women involved in the formal decision-making structure, but it is usually possible. NGO staff need to be aware of the constraints and find creative ways of dealing with some of the potential conflicts. The following example of refugee 'empowerment' with people displaced by conflict in Northern Uganda illustrates the case in point:

'All block leaders were men. The representatives of the implementing agency (food, shelter, etc) worked very closely with refugee committee, pushed hard with them (all women) to get some women block leaders. The first one was an ex-teacher with a family of young children and other dependents. After a few days she came asking me to relieve her of her duties because she was getting too much hassle and did not have time or energy to cope with it. After some discussion, she agreed to persevere. Later, with the Gender Project Officer, we pushed for a system of leaders and deputies — one of which had to be a woman.'

It was not necessarily that men recognised the need to have women in those positions, but rather that they lost interest in the job. 'Men were interested in positions at first because there was no other occupation and as block leaders, they were in charge of distribution of items. But over time, there were increased opportunities for work in a nearby town and the distribution systems were well-established so that the jostling for power period had subsided.'

Psychosocial effects of conflict on women

'Continual exposure to events one can do nothing about frequently results in a psychological state of helplessness. This state of helplessness can include lessening one's perception of control over outcomes, a depression of mood, and a decrease in one's motivation to initiate new responses. Extreme effects of helplessness include fear, anxiety, depression, disease and even death.' (Cohen, p.68 in C.D. Speilberger and I.G. Sarason, 1986)

Much of the current research on stress emphasises the importance of the lack of control or the perception of lack of control being a major factor in stress, even more so than the particular stress factor. 'The feeling of control, the fact or illusion that one can make a personal choice, becomes particularly important in a situation of stress.'[31] Reactions to stress involve various phases: alarm or shock, in which there can be intense emotional discomfort; the resistance phase, which involves the coping efforts to manage the stress; and finally the exhaustion phase, manifested in mental health disorders. Stress reactions should not be considered pathological, but rather as adequate responses to abnormal or threatening situations. Health problems appear when adaptation efforts fail and/or exposure to stress is overwhelming or persistent.

Vulnerability and protective factors affect people's ability to cope with a stressful situation. Factors that increase vulnerability, such as a bad socio-economic situation, tend to increase the effects of stressful situations while protective factors, such as good social networks tend to reduce the impact of stress on mental health. Situations of conflict can exacerbate the vulnerability factors directly, for example, through destitution of means of production and by destroying family and social networks, thus putting people in extreme situations of vulnerability. There are many factors that increase women's vulnerability, not least their lower social and economic status, and it is not difficult to imagine the major impact that conflict can have on their ability to cope with major stress and their multiple responsibilities.

Research conducted with Mozambican refugees in Zambia[32] and Central American (mainly Salvadoran) refugee women in Washington studied the various factors affecting women's response. Some of their findings are as follows:

1 Experience of trauma

Refugee women have been victims of traumatic events, and in addition are subject to daily life events which are stressful. They worry constantly about their situation, and that of their children and family, in addition to having to relive the memories of the trauma they experienced. Women are targeted directly, but also through their children. 'In a context of ongoing violence, the violent death of someone close to you can engender feelings of extreme vulnerability. It constitutes a form of victimisation.' In other words, women may be physically unharmed, but still left psychologically affected. The mental and emotional energy spent in trying to deal with the traumatic life events can hinder the ability to cope with everyday life. Table I summarises the type of events women had experienced.

2 Current stresses

In addition to their direct experience of trauma women face additional worries and concerns such as how to satisfy the basic needs of themselves and their families. The situations that they face, even after they have escaped from direct conflict, are not themselves conducive to healing or resolution of problems. This makes the Western model of counselling individuals within a normal situation, to overcome particular events, of limited value, as most often the situation continues to be an abnormal one. Also, the level of trauma in a community may be so high that this model is simply too costly.

3 Mediating factors

One of the ways in which it is possible to help is by addressing some of the contributing factors, trying to limit or lessen their negative impact, and trying to identify which are the mediating factors that can contribute to lessening this negative impact. The extended family or other social networks can play a useful role. In the study mentioned for Mozambican woman, living with extended family that they perceived as supportive and having friends were factors which contributed to reducing stress, while for the Salvadoran woman this was not available, and so having a good relationship with their partner or husband became the main source of support. (In some cases marriage can cause additional stress for women.) This can also help to identify those who are most at risk in a community. For example, single women, children who have lost both parents, or those with no social support.

4 Gender differences

Being a direct victim of trauma predicted more difficulties. In one study men had been direct victims of violence more often than women, but did not necessarily have more difficulties in coping with everyday life. There are significant differences in the way women and men are affected by current stresses: in the studies, women worried more about family issues such as the relationships with children and husband, whereas men were more concerned with issues like access to health and education.

There were differences in the degree to which women and men are affected, with women being more affected than men, particularly with feelings of helplessness. Also men tended to have greater access to social support, both within and outside the family (see table II). The assumption is that it is the access to a range of support networks rather than a single one that is important. It appears from the table that men have more people to talk to, but also more time at their disposal. Women tend to be more involved in agricultural or household and childcare tasks that leave them little time to make contact with the support networks that are available.

One of the differences in conflict situations is that the whole context is abnormal and the whole social support network is affected. That is, the givers of social support (often the women) are equally under stress and in need of support. In these circumstances it is important to understand well how the networks operate and how they can be strengthened.

5 The children

The emotional well-being of the mother affects the children directly. Studies have shown that children whose mothers had been directly traumatised or were severely emotionally distressed, were more likely to have difficulties. Women can sometimes react by emotional withdrawal, and even neglect their children, as witnessed in refugee camps in Sudan. This also highlights the need when dealing with trauma in children to look at the family, and in particular, the mother.

Conclusions

It is necessary for agencies to look at a whole range of interventions and address the overall concerns of both men and women in conflict. Practical interventions, for example the provision of firewood or other fuel for cooking, health services, etc. can go a long way in terms of decreasing the stress for women.

Summerfield stresses the importance of those who suffer conflict being able to give meaning to and share what they have gone through.[33] The simple provision of a 'refuge' or similar gathering place where people can do this may be of great benefit.[34] To enable or facilitate the healing process NGOs need to be aware of the issues and have a good understanding of the people they are working with.

Fig. 8. *The effects of conflict on women*

Table I. *Percentages of women who were victims of traumatic events*

	Mozambicans	Salvadorans
Witnessed murder	44.0	21.7
Knew someone murdered	60.0	57.7
Injured by violence	11.0	4.5
Rape/Sexually abused	2.8	2.7
Interrogated/detained	12.8	16.2
Tortured	32.1	1.8
Threatened/humiliated by verbal abuse	40.3	13.5
Experienced a house search	39.4	25.2
Forced to participate in military activity	20.2	1.8
Property/cattle taken	41.3	NA
Separated from children	24.0	NA
Present when home/neighbourhood bombed	NA	38.7
Forced to seek safety from gunfire	NA	42.3
Robbed/feared for life on journey to USA	NA	24.3

NA = Not included as a traumatic event for this group

Table II. *Protective Index*

	Men	Women
1. Works	61.8	83.6
2. Married/lives with someone	94.1	66.0
3. Extended family in same household	24.5	22.7
4. Extended family nearby	83.4	57.3
5. Family member who gives emotional support	66.7	71.8
6. Friends	78.4	42.7
7. Religious affiliation	55.9	45.5
8. Someone to talk to if worried	72.5	53.6
9. Member of club/village committee	50.0	17.3
10. Family perceived as a source of support	55.9	49.1
11. Family *not* perceived as a source of stress		77.

Mean score for men   8.19
Mean score for women   6.54

Reference: *The Psychological Well-Being of Refugee Children — Research, Practice and Policy Issues*

WOMEN'S ISSUES IN THE CONTEXT OF OVERT CONFLICT

Case Study 5: A CHECKLIST

Gigi Francisco

1 Women-headed households

Temporary, in the context of displacement until reunited with spouse in original place of residence; or

Permanent, in the context of death of spouse, or resettlement in a far away place without the spouse who may have decided to stay behind in the conflict area or join either of the armed forces

Specific problems

- Increased triple burden as women are left to care for children and the aged.

- Issue of survival/increased marginalisation in a society where the sexual division of labour determines allocation of resources, rights, and opportunities (statistics from Third World countries show that women-headed households tend to be the poorest).

- More vulnerable to sexual abuse (although women who have their spouses around have also been raped, some in front of their defenceless and terrified spouses).

- Mental stress/psychological impact of war and its consequences. Women have to attend to the needs of family members who have been scarred by war even while she, herself, suffers all sorts of stresses and vulnerabilities.

2 Sexual abuse and harassment, in the context of the following:

Within area/community of conflict, during operations (civilians caught in the war, local or international); under interrogation/detention by military; when seeking welfare assistance (e.g. evacuation, food, water, health services).

Forms of sexual abuse/specific problems

- Rape: military/political rape (repeated rape by one man/multiple rape)

- Sexual harassment : threat of sexual abuse
  : humiliation through verbal vulgarities and abuse by men
  : vulnerability to touching of sensitive/private parts by men

- Sexual slavery: in the context of forced, regular sexual favours through mistress system (documented by Gabriela);

- Sexual commodification: military prostitution, as an established institution/ culture of patriarchy;

3 Severe condition of reproduction-related responsibilities among women civilians caught in the midst of military operations/total war tactics and strategies

Specific problems (outside of sexual abuse and harassment, and as women-headed households)

- As food producers, procurers and preparers: increased hardship due to food blockades, no man's land (limited mobility), food quotas, economic constriction, devastation of livestock/crops.

- As household health managers: increased hardship due to bombings and strafing resulting in deaths in the household, deaths of infants and children due to malnutrition and outbreak of epidemics, cutting-off of institutional support, limited mobility.

- As child-carers: unimagined hardship due to all of the above, manages the children during evacuations bombing, etc.

- As pregnant and lactating mothers: malnutrition, physical and emotional stress

4 Women's health

(There is a need to separate this as an issue since most often, it is only the health of children and mothers which is addressed in the context of relief assistance during armed conflicts and in evacuation centres.)

Specific health problems

- Malnutrition among women.

- Maternal health.

- Psychological/emotional stress or instabilities resulting from war and its consequences (death, dislocation, rape, etc.).

- Physical disabilities/illnesses arising from war that make it difficult for women to carry out critical reproductive roles.

- Sexually transmitted diseases and/or viral/bacterial infection: may be due to rape, inadequate/poor sanitation; often overlooked by women themselves; if unattended, may leave to more serious reproduction-related illnesses such as cancer.

Gigi Francisco, Women's Resource and Research Center: April 1991

II. c Meeting the Support Needs of Women in Conflict Situations

6. Case Study: Sri Lanka

Destruction of homes in conflict, Sri Lanka

C MEETING THE SUPPORT NEEDS OF WOMEN IN CONFLICT SITUATIONS

Case Study 6: SRI LANKA

Nalini Kasynathan

Background

Sri Lanka has experienced continuous conflict for more than a decade. The war in the North-East has claimed several tens of thousands of lives, caused extensive damage to infrastructure and led to massive displacement of people. Over one and half million people are displaced within Sri Lanka, of whom 250,000 are living in refugee camps; 50,000 are refugees in Canada; 210,000 in India officially (with an additional unofficial figure of around 150,000); a further 100,000 refugees are in Europe; and 10,000 in Australia.

Currently people continue to be displaced, as villages are attacked by the government security forces, paramilitary groups, Home Guards or militant groups. In October 1992 an attack on four villages in the Polannaruwa district resulted in the massacre of over 200 villagers. This, and the subsequent retaliatory killings, led to a massive outflow of people from this area.

The work of Community Action Abroad (CAA)

1 CAA's work in Sri Lanka

This case study concentrates on the work of Community Aid Abroad (CAA). The CAA-sponsored project on which it focuses is located in the Batticoloa district in Eastern Sri Lanka. Here, major fighting broke out once again in June 1990 between the government forces and militant groups in Batticoloa. This led to 30,000 people fleeing into the surrounding jungle, while 150,000 moved out of their villages to live with friends and relatives in and around the town, and 50,000 entered government-run refugee camps.

CAA started working in Batticaloa in January 1992 with the refugees who were beginning to return after their flight during the June 1990 fighting. While some of these were returning to their homes, there were many others who were newcomers to the area, which they perceived as more secure than their own home regions, from which they had fled. All refugees coming into Batticaloa had lost their homes and livelihoods, while many had additionally lost family members.

2 Initial relief measures

With funding provided by the Australian Government (AIDAB), CAA started a relief and rehabilitation programme for two thousand families. Organising the refugees into groups, the programme provided them with building materials to construct basic shelters, cooking utensils, agricultural implements, seeds and fertilisers.

The programme was not gender-specific and were intended to help the displaced of both sexes to resettle in their new environment. Distribution of protein supplements for mothers and children was an important component of the programme.

3 Moves from relief to economic recovery

The men among these refugees could not find any employment and tended to sit idle, while the women took upon themselves the main burden of sustaining their families: they picked grain from fields harvested the previous year, nursed children who were suffering from malaria, diarrhoea and many other infectious diseases, fetched drinking water and gathered firewood.

At the end of eight months, an evaluation was done to assess the efficiency of aid delivery. The beneficiaries, especially the women, indicated that they would prefer some of the funds allocated for some consumer items to be given instead in the form of loans for agriculture. CAA's partner at this stage was the Dry Zone Development Foundation (DDF), an organisation working in the area on credit programmes.

On the basis of the women's request, CAA agreed to provide more agricultural assistance to the families in the project area. This was particularly concentrated on the women who were found to have taken on the responsibility for the welfare of their families. For this reason vegetable cultivation, rather than paddy (rice farming), was identified as a suitable income-generation activity. It was possible to get the full participation of women in this activity because vegetables were grown around their homestead, and all farming activities, such as watering and tilling of vegetable plots, were manageable by women.

As a result of the cultivation during the first season, many families were able to earn between rupees 1500-2000 after providing for their domestic consumption. On account of this success, the programme was extended to include another 700 families. The families were also provided with the services of agricultural extension officers. They were also provided with training in functional literacy, health education, and the basics of financial management.

After a year of such activity, it was clear that the beneficiaries had grown out of the relief phase of their resettlement. By now there were 47 societies with a total of 1800 members, of which 70 per cent were women. The societies elected a central executive committee to manage the programme. Of the five members of this committee, four were women.

CAA assistance was now provided, once again at the request of the beneficiaries, to establish hand-loom centres, cane handicraft, preservation and processing of agricultural produce, and skills training. At this stage it became evident that the women members were beginning to see inadequacies in the organisation of the DDF which was working with them on the credit programme. The coordinators of the organisation were not easily or readily accessible. The members also felt that they were being excluded from the decision-making process in the organisation. They called a general meeting of the project, and proposed a restructuring whereby the women's groups became direct recipients and managers of project funds. This direct involvement of the women was a main factor in the subsequent growth of the project.

4 Conflict offers women room for manoeuvre

War provides an opportunity for women's empowerment. The challenge is to make women conscious of the empowerment issues here so that the gains made would survive the war.

The disruption by war of established structures, guidelines and taboos has made room for them to move into areas from which they were previously excluded. Even the men who are left in the villages are vulnerable to attack or harassment, and women therefore find themselves having to take on public roles and make the decisions too. They feel less endangered than men in negotiating with the army, officials or with the militants. They take on many non-traditional occupations, including positions in the combat cadres.

5 The chances of sustaining women's empowerment into peacetime

The lesson from other similar situations in the past, including the Second World War, is that women tend to slip back into traditional roles as conflict gives way to peace and the restoration of earlier norms. Attention must therefore be focused on empowerment as an ongoing process through women organising themselves collectively with an understanding of their position as one of exploitation and disempowerment. Work with women must not confine itself to relief and refugee work and to trauma counselling. It must deliberately seek to build on the urgency and the opportunities generated by war. Income-generation activities must be used to build women's organisations which would focus on conscious empowerment.

Conclusions

One must distinguish between the practical difficulties in working in hazardous areas and the suitability or otherwise of income generating and organisational work in war situations. Instead of it being true that only disaster relief work can be done in war situations, CAA's work in Sri Lanka shows that development work may be the only effective way of dealing with the damage caused by protracted war.

Women demonstrated their willingness to engage in such development work and their capacity to plan and organise its nature themselves. Substantial steps were taken towards women empowering themselves in this programme.

Acknowledgement

In writing this case study, I have drawn extensively on factual information in field reports and a paper by Shanthi Sachidananthan, CAA's Project Officer in Sri Lanka.

II. D Working with Partners on Gender Issues in Conflict Situations

    7. Case Study: Burma
    8. Case Study: Philippines

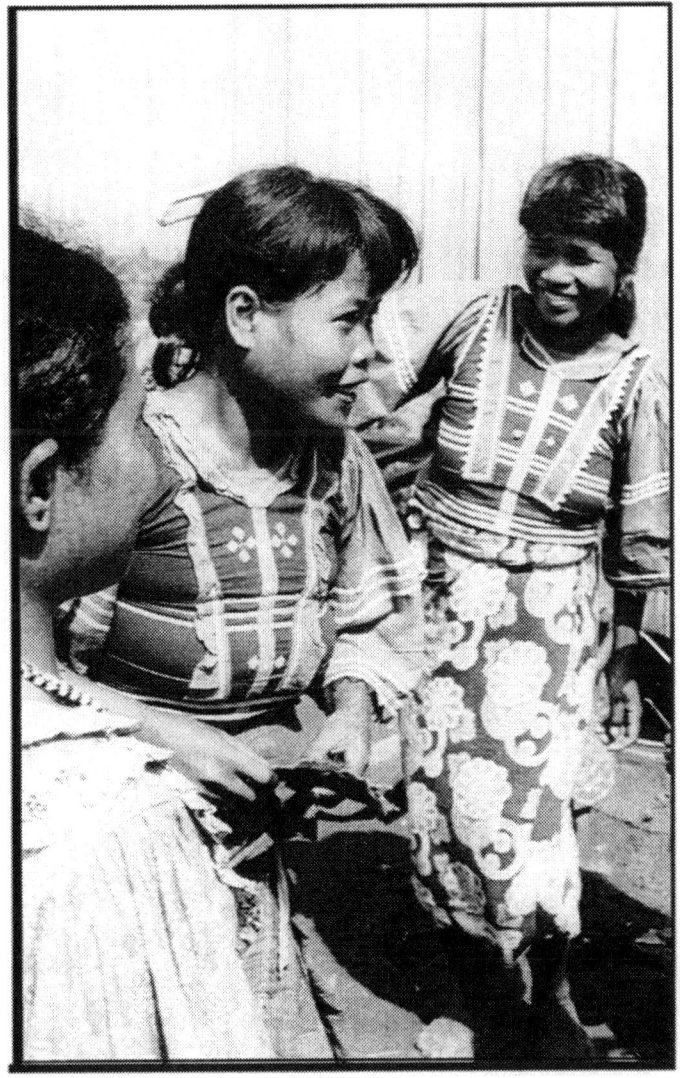

Women from Mindanao, Philippines, singing traditional songs to strengthen their resolve to hold onto their land, threatened by logging

D. WORKING WITH PARTNERS ON GENDER ISSUES IN CONFLICT SITUATIONS

Case Study 7: BURMA

Shona Kirkwood

Background

Burma's political problems started soon after Independence in 1948 when a series of opposition groups went underground. During successive governments, both democratic and military, a number of uprisings took place, with the largest in 1988 being led by students. Thousands were killed or arrested, while around 10,000 fled to the border areas. After pressure from the international community, the government held elections in 1990 which were considered to have produced a fair result. The main opposition party, the NLD, won 85 per cent of the vote, but the junta refused to hand over power. The current situation is a stalemate; however, the government at present has the upper hand, having acquired international support since announcing the elections, notably from logging and oil companies. It is believed that it may soon be in a position to overcome the opposition groups.

The Burmese Relief Centre

The Burmese Relief Centre (BRC) was set up in 1988, originally to help students living around the Thai border. It later started extending assistance to refugees from the Keren ethnic group, who had been in exile or semi-exile since soon after Independence. About 70,000 Burmese refugees now live in camps in Thailand. BRC works through the All Burma Students Democratic Front (ABSDF), the Keren National Union (KNU) and through other member organisations of the Democratic Alliance of Burma (DAB). It works both in camps in Thailand and in areas inside Burma controlled by the resistance forces. Most of BRC's assistance is focused on three elements: emergency provision of food, medicine and clothing, medical training, and education.

Specific problems of women

Within these populations, the particular problems women face are the following:

1 Forced labour

Women are coerced to work as forced labour in construction work or as porters for the Burmese army. Women form about 50 per cent of the labour force in construction work and number one-fifth of all army porters. Survival rates among the latter are extremely low, with illnesses, including malaria, resulting from lack of care and lack of food. Women porters in particular are often subject to nightly gang rape by soldiers.

2 Lack of family planning and pre/postnatal care

Abortion is common and there is much inaccurate knowledge surrounding childbirth.

3 High infant mortality rates

Infant mortality rates are very high. Death claims 50 per cent of under-fives in some of the areas controlled or partially controlled by the resistance.

4 Single parent households

5 Prostitution

40,000 Burmese women are estimated to be working in Thai brothels. Many of these are girls who enter domestic or other sorts of menial service and are later sold into prostitution. The prevalence of AIDS is very high among prostitutes in Thailand and the killing of AIDS victims is not uncommon.

BRC's activities with students and refugees

BRC is able to address some of women's problems, notably 2 and 3 above, but on too small a scale to solve the problems, being restricted both by lack of funds and staff and by the lack of gender awareness within BRC and its partner organisations.

The students and the Keren refugees present two different communities with different gender profiles. Keren refugee women are highly respected and valued by men. They have equal opportunities and often control the family budget. There is a death sentence in cases of rape. Yet Keren women face many problems which the current political organisations are not dealing with, since there are few women at the higher levels of the organisation. For example, despite women being 52 per cent of the Keren population, there are only 5 women out of 45 in the central committee of the Keren National Union (KNU). Women tend to feel satisfied with their present role and do not want to challenge men.

The Keren Women's Organisation was in fact set up by the president of the KNU, with the intention of bringing women into the political struggle, rather than at the instigation of Keren women themselves. The KWO is thus an arm of the KNU, to whom its policy is subordinated; KNU policy is set up by men and women are not consulted in the process. The KWO is also disadvantaged financially, receiving around 10 per cent of the movement's (diminishing) income while the KNU receives 90 per cent.

The Burman student population, around 2,500 of them living in 22 camps on the Thai-Burma border, have a somewhat different composition, since women form less than 10 per cent of this population. Most students have sought refuge as individuals rather than families, and women have proved reluctant to cut themselves off from their families to the same degree as men. Commitment to the revolutionary struggle is a strong part of the students' motivation, in addition to fear of reprisals from the government.

Women among the students tend to feel they have no significant role in the struggle (there are no women on the central committee) and their morale is low as a result. In addition, they face many health problems and, having no knowledge about or access to contraception, suffer many pregnancies. The women students have limited occupational options; those with education may become teachers or nurses, while those without tend to be cooks or cleaners. However, one woman has recently received training in women's development and may soon begin to change things.

Conclusions

For women's needs to be addressed as a higher priority, much groundwork needs to be done in raising gender awareness among all parties, as well as strengthening women's representation within the political structures: for example by strengthening the KWO, by increasing the number of women in the KNU central committee, and by promoting a women's movement within the ABSDF. However, this issue is currently clouded by the serious military situation in which the rebel movements find themselves. Given the overwhelming need for enhancing the military position of the refugees, is this the moment to start working for greater gender equality?

On the one hand, women stand to gain considerably from a Keren victory (in terms of freedom from gross abuses such as slave labour and, in the longer term perhaps, prostitution). Because of this, maintaining the military integrity of the movement is a priority for women as well as for men.

On the other hand, the refugees' survival depends not only on military strength but also on the strengthening of the community's coping mechanisms, which are in fact being eroded by the inability to address gender issues. It is perhaps exactly at this critical time, when all established patterns of behaviour are threatened with radical change, that gender most needs to be addressed.

In situations where gross discrimination is practised against a particular group, for example on ethnic or political grounds, the goal of gender equality within that group may appear to some to be subordinate to the needs of the political and military struggle, which aims to create the conditions for empowerment of the whole community. But enabling all sections of the community to contribute to that struggle as fully as possible is also a vital survival strategy for the whole population. Times of crisis provide opportunities for change.

Helping resistance organisations to become aware of the gender dimensions to their struggle may be a timely contribution by outside support agencies.

Case Study 8: THE PHILIPPINES

PSYCHOSOCIAL SUPPORT IN CONFLICT

Arlene C Mahinay

Attending to the psychosocial needs and problems of people — specially women in situations of armed conflict — is a relatively new field of disaster response in the Philippines. While more and more NGOs are now aware of the great need to address the problem, the majority are still in the process of coming up with a concept and a comprehensive view on how to concretely respond to the psychosocial effects of conflict.

Only a few groups have gone beyond the research and conceptualisation stage and have begun to implement direct programmes with psychosocial services. Yet even these advanced groups still have to emerge from the 'infancy stage' of psychosocial work. Currently, each of them is groping its way amid problems associated with lack of human resources, lack of funds, and lack of experience to guide them ahead.

If psychosocial work in general is as yet an emerging field, then much more so are psychosocial services directed towards the particular circumstances of women in situations or armed conflict.

However, a few groups have already begun to establish mechanisms in response to this. These include some women's groups at the national level. Already hampered by the problems mentioned above, these women's NGOs also have to contend with a male-oriented and male-dominated atmosphere which tends to refuse to acknowledge women's needs and concerns.

Nevertheless, despite major limitations, hopes are high among these women's NGOs that this field of disaster response will achieve a higher level of effectiveness in the future. They, together with other advocates, are raising several issues that if addressed, they believe, would enable the groups working on the psychosocial effects of armed conflict to significantly advance their work.

Psychosocial effects of armed conflict on women in the Philippines

The most obvious effect of armed confrontation between government troops and rebels is the massive displacements of communities, causing serious economic and psychosocial problems. Women are particularly vulnerable in this situation.

1 Women as family carers

Data from NGOs show the extent of armed conflict-related traumas suffered by women. Emotional distress and anxiety are caused by physical and economic displacement, specially in women-headed households. Experience of disaster-response NGOs show that women act as both father and mother in most situations of armed conflict. Having to take care of the children, they face the additional burden of ensuring that the family has enough food to eat.

On top of this, women constitute the majority of volunteers for disaster-response groups. As such, they take part in registering disaster victims, acting as disaster-response committee members, attending training sessions and acting as negotiating panel for peace talks with warring groups.

Women have to perform all these activities at the same time as they are trying to cope with the emotional stress of being physically separated from their husbands, who may be in hiding for fear of being suspected as a rebel, or may be combatants.

The fact that women comprise the majority of disaster volunteer workers reflects a gender bias not only at community level, but within the NGO as well. Many NGOs believe that women are easier to mobilise for disaster response because, firstly, they are not tied to production work. Secondly, disaster response is viewed as women's work; thirdly, women are more committed to service because of their innate and natural gift for nurturing and mothering.

The distress of having to perform all these roles is often expressed in psychosomatic illnesses. Women in evacuation centres, for example, usually complain of recurring headaches, or body pains and dizziness, without any identified medical cause.

2 Women victims of torture

Because women are the more visible sex in the community during conflict, having to do all the parenting and volunteering for community work and associated tasks, women are particularly vulnerable to extreme human rights abuses. Women constitute the majority of Direct Service Workers (DSWs) in the Philippines, and reports of their harassment are common. At times, DSWs are used as human shields: in Masbate and Ifugao, women DSWs were made to stay with soldiers in one room for about a week, to thwart any attempt by rebels to raid the building.

3 Women victims of rape

Apart from non-gender-specific physical torture, women are also vulnerable to rape and other forms of sexual abuse and harassment. Cases of women being raped before being killed are not uncommon.

Cases of women being used as 'comfort women' occur. For example, in the Masbate and Ifugao incidents, the DSWs involved state that the soldiers who stayed with them in the one room made several drunken attempts to rape them.

Past experience with conflict of a civil war scale in the Philippines have also shown that rape at times appears to become part of the war strategy. During the Muslim war (in the southern part of the Philippines) in the 1970s, warring groups raped enemy women as a way of revenging themselves on their foes.

Response to psychosocial trauma

1 Community support systems

At the community level there are rarely any support systems provided for those suffering from psychosocial effects of conflict. Communities not only lack the professional capacity to assist, but also focus their attention on the more basic concern of ensuring that children are safe from physical harm during the emergency situation.

2 State support systems

On the part of the government, most agencies offering help to displaced communities do not consider assisting psychosocial cases as part of their work. Hence, apart from sometimes bringing a patient directly to the mental hospital, the problem is normally ignored.

3 The role of NGOs

Even among NGOs working in the Philippines, fewer than ten have, in the last couple of years, set up services at the national level to combat the harmful psychological effects of armed conflict. Only about two or three of these programmes deal specifically with women victims. The rest are not gender sensitive and have no gender perspective in their programmes.

Type of psychosocial support services extended

The few NGOs that work on psychosocial problems resulting from armed conflict have not gone beyond the preliminary level of such work. Except on gender issues, these groups use similar approaches and methods in their work, which include the following:

- tension relaxation training, aimed at relieving psychosomatic symptoms of patients;
- individual counselling and group counselling to patients.
- group dynamics among patients;
- individual and group counselling of relatives;
- sessions with community members.

All these are aimed at relieving the tension of the patient or patients, as well as providing an atmosphere conducive to restoring mental equilibrium. Staff running these programmes are mainly psychologists. For extreme cases, the services of consultant psychiatrists are also used. However, problems often occur since most patients oppose the idea of seeing psychiatrists, associating the idea of psychiatry with losing one's mind.

Problems faced by these groups generally focus on the lack of human resources, lack of experience and reference materials to guide them ahead, and financial constraints. Among those who attempt to respond to women's psychosocial problems, additional constraints are faced, one of which is the lack of gender-sensitive psychiatrists in the country at present.

Gender-related problems also crop up during therapy or counselling sessions for relatives or community. Men usually view counselling sessions as suitable only for women, and so do not attend and actively participate in these activities. Taking care of the patient is also seen as the task of the wife or mother.

Conclusions

There is currently a dearth of information on the impact of armed conflict on women, including the psychosocial effects of war. Data on this would facilitate essential work, such as training curriculum development, programme planning, and awareness raising.

There is an acute need to incorporate gender perspectives, issues, and concerns in conflict-related disaster response and in other fields of community work. Only a few NGOs are addressing the specific problems of women victims of armed conflict. This is not only true in the psychosocial field but also in relief and rehabilitation. NGOs generally do not make specific provisions for women in relief and rehabilitation work, despite the fact that women have expressed particular needs during emergency situations, while displacement often places an increased burden on them.

This is not to say that most NGOs do not have some awareness of the value of gender analysis in development. However, the majority lack the necessary knowledge and skills to take definite steps in integrating gender into their programmes and services. In this situation, gender training is definitely required.

There is a need to recognise mental health as an issue, and a need to correct misconceptions about mental health. There is a tendency for people, even health workers, to ignore or not to recognise or acknowledge mental health concerns. Community and even health workers, tend to look at people's disaster-related problems in terms of physical and economic needs only. Hardly anybody looks into the disaster's effects on the people's mental and/or emotional well-being, and people judged to have mental problems are stigmatised. Although this trend has started to be overturned now with more people realising the need to examine the emotional and mental health of disaster victims, increased efforts have to be made in this area.

There is a great need for NGOs to exert efforts to correct misconceptions and other myths surrounding mental health. One difficulty expressed by psychosocial workers is the patient's reluctance to be referred to psychiatrists. They associate psychiatry with having 'gone crazy'. Even their relatives express negative reactions at the idea for fear of the attached stigma. People should be helped to recognise and value the role of psychiatry in mental health.

One of the limitations of the current work being done in the country is the inability of NGOs to set up psychosocial support mechanism at the community level. This should be done to supplement the prevailing clinical approach, a limitation of which is the reality that there are more patients than there are psychologists to attend to them, and that success of treatment could be boosted when there is a mechanism at the community level to do follow up work. Psychosocial impact of any armed hostility may be lessened with the timely proactive intervention of a community-based structure.

These issues may not only be relevant in the Philippines but in other countries also rocked by internal strife. Oxfam may play a significant role not only in supporting the development of psychosocial responses, but in ensuring the presence of a gender perspective as well. Support may range from providing financial assistance to sharing technical expertise. In our experience, the simple act of consistently asking about the particular needs of women disaster victims led to a partner's initiative to add a session on gender issues in one training programme.

Women victims of sexual abuse during conflict should be encouraged to come out into the open to receive therapy. People should be informed about the issue to erase stigma and biases. There are now several groups working toward this end, although they do not specifically deal with those victimised in armed conflict. As a result perhaps of the efforts of these groups, a growing number of Filipino women have publicly related their traumatic experiences and thus contributed to the public's education on the issue of sexual abuse.

It is hoped that the combined efforts of the affected communities, NGOs, and agencies such as Oxfam, will result in the improved psychosocial state of women caught up in situations of armed conflict.

II. E The Evolution of Oxfam's Gender Strategy in Conflict

9. Lebanon

Women participating in the rebuilding of Ain el Hilweh Palestinian refugee camp, Sidon

E. THE EVOLUTION OF OXFAM'S GENDER STRATEGY IN CONFLICT

Case Study 9: LEBANON

Lina Abu Habib

Oxfam's role in Lebanon has evolved in response to the general situation in the country, and in particular to the way the Lebanese NGO' which Oxfam supports have developed their own response to the unfolding conflict. Factors internal to Oxfam have also played a significant part in determining the policies and actions of Oxfam in the Lebanon.

This evolution can be seen by looking at four periods of significance in the progress of the war:

1 The Israeli invasion, which took place in 1982 and which led in 1983 to the war on the southern suburbs of Beirut.

2 The Israeli withdrawal from the mountains and parts of South Lebanon was progressive, extended over the period 1984-87, and precipitated the Camps War (Palestinians versus Palestinians, Lebanese versus Palestinians), the Mountains War (Druze versus Christians), and the East of Saida War (Christians versus leftist militias). There was massive, long-term displacement of population as a result of these conflicts.

3 The height of the Lebanese war of 1989-90, in which more than half the country was affected by intense and devastating fighting with huge numbers of casualties.

4 The period following the 1990 peace treaty in which security was restored and political and economic reform has been under discussion.

The first of these periods saw the establishment of an Oxfam office in the country running an emergency programme through local NGOs and UNRWA. It is hard to tell how far Oxfam was attuned to gender issues at this time since little documentation survives, but gender was not generally seen as an issue then, either within Oxfam or among the partner NGOs.

Some women's groups did exist, often affiliated, as the KWO in Burma, to political parties — and the majority of NGO field staff were women; however, decision-making was largely in the hands of men. The priority of the NGOs was to cope with the social repercussion of the invasion.

During the second period Oxfam began to focus on a number of non-confessional NGOs, supporting the work they were doing in the fields of relief and rehabilitation and social services, together with primary health care. NGOs — and especially secular ones — were facing pressure exerted by de facto militia powers (which are necessarily sectarian), and Oxfam's aim was to help them survive. A substantial number of projects supported dealt with women, and employment of a part-time gender PO was contemplated. The war and economic situation had given rise to an increasing number of female-headed households and many NGOs were starting to work with women on, for example, child care and income-generation projects. Though the Oxfam office recognised the need to look at women in development (WID) issues, it did not have the skills to deal with them, and these were in any case obscured by the pressures of the emergency situation.

The third period (civil war) could be characterised as 'business as usual' for Oxfam, which continued to support NGOs and their work in relief at community level. Despite the intensity of the war, Oxfam's programme was oriented towards development projects while maintaining some emergency intervention. However, the Oxfam office began to think about carrying out a review of the programme's basic assumptions. As far as gender was concerned, WID was definitely recognised as an issue by this time: partner NGOs recognised women as a main target group in this conflict situation, and Oxfam made deliberate attempts to involve women in project-related discussions. However, women's issues were on the whole addressed at the level of individual projects, and no formal gender analysis had appeared at this stage.

During the latest stage, internal factors had a greater bearing on developments. Oxfam's strategic planning process was in place, and within the Lebanon, Oxfam began discussions with partners on rethinking their and Oxfam's strategies and identifying for the first time a coherent shape and direction for the Lebanon programme. Gender and the environment emerged as main themes in the future programme, helped both by the Gender and Development Unit (GADU) incorporating gender into the strategic planning process, and by the NGOs' awareness of the term. This awareness coincided with an increased interest by donor agencies in promoting gender as a condition of funding.

The present situation is that political and economic reform and the optimism of the Middle East peace process is coinciding with Oxfam's first year of strategic planning. Gender training and a new gender analysis within the country's own context are in process, and gender will be promoted within a joint review with partners. The atmosphere within Oxfam is now conducive to gender work and there is a consensus on gender within the Lebanon office. The peace process provides some space to discuss gender issues, even though it may ultimately not succeed. Lebanese NGOs are having to consider their position on gender issues very carefully, partly because of the increasing conditionality of donor agencies who believe the Lebanon is no longer an emergency situation, and partly because they — like Oxfam — will soon have to analyse the implications and causes of the rise of fundamentalism, and the effect it might have on gender relations and the situation of women in the country and the region.

Conclusions

In the Lebanon, the growth of local NGOs has been closely linked to the course of the war and the emergency needs of the people.

Oxfam's view of its role has been oriented towards developing the capacity of its counterparts to cope with growing political, social, and economic problems and helping to ensure their survival through very difficult times, and this gives Oxfam the credibility to raise new issues such as gender in a positive environment.

Gender awareness in Oxfam and its partners has been stimulated by the socio-economic changes in Lebanon, and also encouraged by institutional factors within Oxfam.

In order to promote discussion of gender issues among its partners, Oxfam recognises the need first to equip its own staff with appropriate skills.

REFERENCES

1 Derek Summerfield, 'The psychosocial effects of conflict in the Third World', *Development in Practice* Vol 1 No 3, 1991.
2 Catherine Bennett,'Ordinary madness', *Guardian*, January 1993.
3 Press reports of rape in former Yugoslavia, 1993.
4 Ibid.
5 Rosanna Carrillo, *Violence against women: an obstacle to development*, New York, Centre for Women's Global Leadership, 1991.
6 Ed Vulliamy, 'Pope warns raped women on abortion', *Guardian*, 1 March 1993.
7 Bennett op.cit.
8 Cécile Mukaruguba, ACORD, personal communication.
9 Chris McGreal, 'Renamo conceals child "brides" of boy soldiers', *Guardian* 11 June 1993.
10 Derek Summerfield, 'The psychological effects of conflict in the third world: a short study', Oxfam 1990.
11 Oxfam Health Unit, 'Effects of conflict on women'. (Paper prepared for gender and conflict workshop.)
12 Ibid.
13 Bennett op.cit.
14 'Eritrean women — the beginning of a new struggle', *African World Review* May-Oct 1993.
15 Eugenia Piza-Lopez, personal account of observations in El Quiche, Guatemala.
16 Karl Maier, 'Women fall victim to Somalia's prejudice', *Independent*, 5 January 1993.
17 Vulliamy, op.cit.
18 Ibid.
19 Women's Caucus document, UN Conference on Human Rights, Vienna, 1993.
20 CCIC/Match *Two halves make a whole*, Ottawa, 1991; Mary B Anderson et al *A framework for people-oriented planning in refugee situations taking account of women, men and children*, UNHCR 1992.
21 Mary B Anderson and Peter Woodrow, *Rising from the ashes*, Westview Press/UNESCO 1989.
22 Sara Hlupekile Longwe, 'Gender Awareness: the missing element in the third world development project', *Changing Perceptions*, Oxfam 1991.
23 See for example Bridget Walker 'Disaster relief: the gender perspective', Oxfam 1993.
24 N Kelley, *Working with refugee women: a practical guide*, NGO Working Group on Refugee Women, 1989.
25 *UNHCR policy on refugee women*. Submitted by the High Commissioner to the Executive Committee of the High Commissioner's Programme.
26 Elizabeth Ferris *Women, war and peace: an issue paper*, Life and Peace Institute, Uppsala 1992.
27 Linda Agerbak 'Breaking the cycle of violence', *Development in practice* Vol.1 No.3, 1991.

28 N Kelley, *Working with Refugee Women: A Practical Guide*, Geneva: NGO Working Group on Refugee Women.
29 Elizabeth Ferris, 'Refugee Women and Family Life', in McCallin M (ed), *The Psychological Well-Being of Refugee Children: Research, Practice and Policy Issues*, ICCB, Geneva.
30 UNHCR Technical Support Services, *UNHCR and Refugee Women*. February 1989.
31 A Mahjoub 'The Theory of Stress As An Approach to Studying Psychological Responses in a War Environment', in McCallin M (ed) *The Psychological Well-Being of Refugee Children: Research, Practice and Policy Issues*, ICCB, Geneva.
32 M McCallin and S Fozzard, *The Impact of Traumatic Events on the Psychological Well-Being of Mozambican Refugee Women and Children*, International Catholic Child Bureau, Geneva, 1990. (Summary by N. Taylor in Health Unit).
33 Derek Summerfield 'Charting Human Response to Extreme Violence and the Limitations of Western Psychiatric Models: An Overview'. Presented in ISTSS World Conference: Trauma and Tragedy. Amsterdam June 1992.
34 Derek Summerfield, 'Psychosocial Effects of Conflict in the Third World: A Short Study', Oxfam, 1990.

www.ingramcontent.com/pod-product-compliance
Ingram Content Group UK Ltd.
Pitfield, Milton Keynes, MK11 3LW, UK
UKHW050226150426
5217IPUK00023B/1672